Songs of DELIVERANCE

Our soul has
escaped
as a bird
from the snare....
Psalm 124:7

Debra Griffin Mitchell

World Video Bible School®

WVBS Publishing
25 Lantana Lane
Maxwell, Texas 78656

Web Address: www.wvbs.org

Email: biblestudy@wvbs.org

Copyright © 2014

ISBN: 9780989431149

Printed in the USA

Print Layout by Aubrie Deaver

Serving the Church since 1986

Table of Contents

Chapter 1: The Song of Moses and Miriam...9

Chapter 2: The Song of Deborah and Barak..17

Chapter 3: The Song of Hannah..25

Chapter 4: The Song of David, Part 1..31

Chapter 5: The Song of David, Parts 2 and 3, Conclusion...........................39

Chapter 6: David's Song of Suffering and Salvation: Psalm 22, Part 1.......47

Chapter 7: David's Song of Suffering and Salvation: Psalm 22, Part 1 continued and Part 2.........................53

Chapter 8 : The Song of Jonah..59

Chapter 9: Deliverance in Captivity...67

Chapter 10: The Song of Mary; Song of the Heavenly Host; Song of Simeon........................75

Chapter 11: The Song of Zacharias...81

Chapter 12: Songs of the Early Church..87

Chapter 13: Five Songs of Heaven in Revelation..93

Dedication

To the glory of God and His Son, Jesus the Christ, with gratitude for Deliverance

Foreword

"What shall we study?" Finding a fresh and challenging topic is the daunting task faced quarterly by every Bible teacher! In *Songs of Deliverance,* Debra Mitchell has created an intensively biblical and unique new course of study.

With skill and research-backed insights, she personalizes the beloved stories of God's heroes of old such as Deborah, Hannah, and David. Then she intimately dissects the songs of gratitude that flowed from their hearts when God delivered them. As those who practice and love a cappella singing, we especially should enjoy probing the depths of the songs of gratitude written by those who came before us—songs that were chosen by God to be preserved in the Bible.

Songs of Deliverance doesn't stop there, however. It goes beyond the milk to the meat when each chapter shows that not only does God provide the deliverance we need but that He delivers us *from* one thing *into* another, thus making this a challenging and beneficial study for all of us.

Sandra Humphrey

Former Editor, *Christian Woman* Magazine

December 2013

Introduction

Deliverance: rescue from danger, defeat, or suffering; release from bondage; relief or freedom from dread or fear. We all need it. We create images to describe it: light at the end of the tunnel; dawn after midnight anxiety; feast after famine. We pray for deliverance in hospitals and funeral homes, in moral dilemmas and so-called hopeless situations.

When our question is "Why?" and we cannot find an answer, the prayer spoken by our tears is, "Deliver me, O Lord."

When Eve and then Adam tasted forbidden fruit, God punished them, but He also promised deliverance from sin (Genesis 3:1-15). This promise affects every major character and event in the Bible; it surfaces in stories of physical and spiritual deliverance for individuals, families, and nations. When wickedness prevails, when fear controls, when hope fades, those in despair call on God to rescue them—and God delivers. Righteousness triumphs, fear fades, and hope flourishes because God keeps His promise (2 Peter 3:9).

Why God Delivers

God's deliverance often has the dual purpose of physical rescue and spiritual enlightenment. He wants to rescue and save, but He also wants us to know who is in charge so the world will know who He is. Therefore, God's deliverance may include not only deliverance *from* danger but also surrender *to* God's will.

For example, God delivered (surrendered) the wicked world *to* punishment of flood waters in Genesis 6, but He saved the righteous man Noah and his family *from* the flood—actually rescuing them by the same means (water) that He used to punish the wicked. Centuries later, God delivered David *from* Goliath, but He also delivered Goliath *to* David (1 Samuel 17:42-50). David had no illusions of self-glory: "The battle is the LORD's, and He will give you into our hands" (v. 47).

Is God egotistical? No, but He is God, the great I Am, Creator and Sustainer of the universe. God created mankind and instilled within each person elements of intelligence, creativity, and even genius, but He did not make us self-sufficient. He created us in His image and intended to have a loving, sacred relationship with us. Whether we acknowledge it or not, we are dependent on Him.

By sinning, Adam and Eve traded their daily fellowship with God for painful knowledge of mortality. They swapped innocence for guilt and an idyllic garden for fields of thorns and death, all because they followed their own desires. They discovered that without God, the world is dreary, dangerous, and desolate.

But God did not leave them desolate, and He does not leave us desolate, either. Throughout the Bible as well as today, God continues to deliver the righteous and teach the wicked, hoping that all will turn from sin, acknowledge His love, and obey His commands.

Responding to Deliverance

In the Bible, patriarchs, prophets, kings, and godly men and women often turned to God for deliverance from physical and spiritual peril. How did they respond to God when He rescued them? Surely divine deliverance demands a response, doesn't it? They thanked God and praised His power and mercy, often in song. By faithful words and deeds, they also pointed to the greatest Deliverer, Jesus the Christ, who still delivers (saves, redeems, rescues) us from the most deadly threats of all—enslavement to sin and eternity in a devil's hell (Colossians 1:13; 1 Thessalonians 1:10).

The Bible doesn't record a song for every act of deliverance, but the songs preserved demonstrate attitudes that Christians today should imitate. When we consider the magnitude of our sin and the grace of God's deliverance from it, we should express gratitude, sacrifice, and praise.

After the Song

Today, Christians do express gratitude for salvation and other forms of deliverance with songs of thanksgiving and praise. Still, salvation and the promise of an eternal home with God surely deserve more than words of praise, however beautifully we may sing those songs. After the sighs of relief and gratitude, after the melody fades to memory, we who have been rescued should strive to maintain our state of deliverance.

Paul asked, "How shall we who died to sin live any longer in it?" (Romans 6:2). In reference to the Israelites, Paul also wrote, "Now all these things happened to them as examples, and they were written for our admonition, upon whom the ends of the ages have come. Therefore he who thinks he stands take heed lest he fall" (1 Corinthians 10:11-12).

The songs remind us of miraculous, undeserved rescue, but they also warn us that God's deliverance continues beyond the initial rescue. When delivered *from* danger and death, Bible heroes were also delivered *to* an opportunity to serve God. "Think about it:"

- Saved *from* the flood, Noah and his family were charged with repopulating and governing the earth (Genesis 9:1-5).

- By delivering the Israelites *from* slavery, Moses also delivered them *to* God's covenant, law, and the Promised Land.

- God sent His Son Jesus to deliver those who accepted Him *from* sin and eternal destruction. The first-century church responded with such joy and zeal that they turned the world upside-down.

- Christians delivered *from* sin were often delivered *to* persecution; their very lives became songs of deliverance, leading to further deliverance and greater zeal.

Paul's plea to his brethren in Rome echoes through the centuries as a challenge for Christians today:

". . . present your bodies a living sacrifice, holy, acceptable to God, which is your reasonable service . . . do not be conformed to this world, but be transformed by the renewing of your mind, that you may prove what is that good and acceptable and perfect will of God" (Romans 12:1-2).

Deliverance does not stop with a sigh of relief when disaster is averted. It does not stop with a sincere, grateful prayer or a song of praise. Those delivered will continue to sing their joy and gratitude by transformed lives that ever seek to imitate the Deliverer.

Chapter 1
The Song of Moses and Miriam
Exodus 15:1-21

A Mother's Love

Jochebed nursed her new son, singing soft praises to God. How blessed she and her husband Amram were, in these troubled times, to have three healthy children: Miriam, Aaron, and now this new little son. But Pharaoh's decree that all Hebrew baby boys must be thrown into the river terrified her. What if soldiers came to take her infant? What could she, a slave, do?

For three months, she hid him, praying for wisdom. Then she decided to entrust the baby to God by way of the inborn desire to nurture and protect one's child that must surely abide even in a pagan woman's heart.

Jochebed wove an ark of bulrushes and covered it with pitch. Calling her daughter Miriam, she took the ark to the river and placed it on the shallow water among the reeds. She told Miriam what to do and went home, leaving them in God's hands.

Miriam guarded the baby and waited. Soon she heard voices; then Pharaoh's daughter appeared with her maids. Seeing the ark, the princess asked, "What is that?" A maid brought the ark and held it as the princess opened it and gasped, "A baby!" As he cried, she felt sorry for him. "This must be a Hebrew child."

Quickly Miriam approached. "Shall I call a nurse from the Hebrew women, to nurse the child for you?"

The princess replied, "Go;" Miriam brought Jochebed. Pharaoh's daughter told her, "I will pay you to nurse him, but when he is older, he will be my son." Jochebed agreed, reaching for him. The princess continued, "I will call him Moses, the word for 'drawn out.'"

Jochebed took her son and nursed him. The king had decreed death by drowning for Hebrew baby boys, but his daughter had saved this one from the water. (Based on Exodus 2:1-10; Numbers 26:29).

Just Thinking . . .

1. Jochebed's actions show her determination to save her baby. What does that suggest about her devotion to God? Was Moses saved by Pharaoh's daughter or by God? Does God have "plans" for people? Consider Jeremiah 29:11 in regard to God's people in captivity as well as Acts 9:10-16 and 2 Peter 3:9.

2. Centuries after Moses, another king massacred all males under age two in Bethlehem, hoping to kill Baby Jesus (Matthew 2:16-18). We might think, "How barbaric!" Yet examples of harshness toward babies exist in modern times. Research China's "one-child policy" and America's "abortion on demand." How should Christians respond to these issues?

Inspiration

To appreciate a deliverance song, we must understand its inspiration. Moses began life as the child of slaves and became the son of Pharaoh's daughter. He had a bi-cultural education, learning Hebrew history from his birth parents and Egyptian history from his adopted mother. He experienced palace luxuries and poverty made rich with spiritual teaching by godly parents. How else could he have chosen "to suffer affliction with the people of God than to enjoy the passing pleasures of sin," (Hebrews 11:23-27), and then forsake Egypt until God called him to deliver His people?

The Song of Moses and Miriam had its roots in the history of Jacob's sons who fathered the twelve tribes of Israel. They moved to Egypt to survive a seven-year famine and stayed 400 years. Favored by Pharaoh because their brother Joseph was the king's second-in-command, they prospered in Goshen. Even after Jacob and his sons died, their descendants lived comfortably. They "increased abundantly . . . and grew exceedingly mighty; and the land was filled with them" (Exodus 1:6-7). Their prosperity demonstrated God's care and blessings as well as His promise to Abraham to make him a great nation (Genesis 12:2).

Contented, they forgot Joseph's dying words: "God will surely visit you, and bring you out of this land to the land of which He swore to Abraham, to Isaac, and to Jacob" (Genesis 50:24). Why think about an ancient promise of a land beyond Egypt, beyond their collective memory, when life was comfortable and pleasant?

New King, New Order

Times changed; a new Pharaoh came to power. The Bible records that he "did not know Joseph" (Exodus 1:8). The Hebrew word translated "know" in this verse is "yada," a verb with shades of meaning more subtle than the English "to know." It includes awareness of facts or abstract concepts, and it is often translated as a reference to sexual union, but in certain contexts, it refers to "an act involving concern, inner engagement, dedication, or attachment to a person. It also means to have sympathy, pity, or affection for someone."[1]

Because of Joseph's accomplishments, any succeeding king would have known who Joseph was, but this Pharaoh had no affection or respect for him. He also feared Joseph's numerous descendants.

"What if we have a war? These people might join our enemies," he thought. So he "afflicted" them as slaves to build his supply cities, making their lives "bitter with hard bondage." Still they multiplied; the Egyptians lived "in dread of the children of Israel" (Exodus 1:9-14). He ordered Hebrew midwives to kill newborn boys; when that failed, he ordered all Hebrew male babies to be cast into the river (1:15-22).

The result was emotional and cultural whiplash. Imagine privileged people suddenly plunged into slavery, conscripted to hard labor, and ordered to murder their baby sons. Imagine years of praying, "God, send us a Deliverer," not realizing he was among them. Moses' first attempt to help the enslaved ended in disaster (Exodus 2:11-15), but God worked through him to deliver the Israelites 40 years later.

Delivered at Last!

When God called Moses to deliver His people, He gave two reasons: "I know their sorrows," and "I have come down . . . to bring them up from that land to a good and large land, a land flowing with milk and honey" (Exodus 3:7-8). The time had come to honor His promise to Abraham.

Through Moses and Aaron, God demonstrated His power with horrible plagues that ended with the death of the firstborn in every Egyptian home. At last, hard-hearted Pharaoh conceded defeat and told Moses to take the people and go (Exodus 12:30-33).

---

1   Abraham J. Heschel, *The Prophets* (Peabody, Mass.: Prince Press, an imprint of Hendrickson Publishers, 2001) 57.

Imagine joy and relief when the Passover feast became physical and spiritual deliverance, when 600,000 men plus families plundered Egypt and marched triumphantly out of bondage. How excited they must have been when they camped beside the Red Sea.

Pharaoh's Last Stand

Back in Egypt, however, Pharaoh had second thoughts. How could he have let Moses bully him into releasing his main labor force? Who would build his cities? Who would respect a king who allowed slaves to leave without a fight? Quickly, he assembled his army, certain of victory (Exodus 14:5-9). The Israelites, trudging through the wilderness with carts, herds, and families, would be helpless before him.

Perhaps the Israelites heard the Egyptians before they saw them. Perhaps the ground trembled from the pounding of horse hooves and chariot wheels; then they "lifted their eyes." As the enemy approached, ". . . they were very afraid, and . . . cried out to the LORD." Freedom turned to panic beside the Red Sea (Exodus 14:10-11).

Then—deliverance! "Stand still, and see the salvation of the Lord . . . the Lord will fight for you" (Exodus 14:13-14). Moses extended the rod; the waters divided; the Israelites "went into the midst of the sea on the dry ground" (14:16, 22). When they were safe on the other side, they watched Egypt's army perish as the sea returned to its place. Then they "feared the LORD, and believed the LORD and His servant Moses" (14:17-31).

The Response

How did the people react? Such deliverance demands celebration, so Moses wrote his song, inspired by God's great work, and taught it to the Israelites. A song is basically a lyric or poem set to music. Instead of rhyme, Hebrew poems employ parallelism, which expresses an idea in the first line and then repeats it in a slightly different way in the second line. Sometimes the second line provides a contrast or expansion of the first line. Images are also important; the writer may describe the same event with several different word pictures to emphasize the impact of God's power.

A song of deliverance has at least three purposes. First, it glorifies and exalts God. Second, it expresses the feelings of an individual or group of witnesses to God's mighty works. Finally, it commemorates and preserves the glory and gratitude associated with those works. Those who witnessed the parting of the Red Sea would teach their children and grandchildren to honor God's deliverance by singing this song, ensuring future generations would marvel and remember the Source of their blessings.

Thousands of years later, we, the spiritual descendants of Abraham and spiritual heirs of the promised Messiah, can read the song of Moses and Miriam and see by faith that glorious deliverance.

Just Thinking . . .

1. As you read the song, underline examples of parallelism and imagery. How do these techniques help us to visualize God's amazing accomplishment at the Red Sea?

2. Parallelism is also an aid to memorization. Why was it important for the Israelites to memorize this song? What are the benefits of memorizing Scripture today?

The Song of Moses and Miriam

Consider now the beauty and structure of this song in Exodus 15. The first stanza consists of verses 1-12; the second stanza consists of verses 13-18. Stanza 1, verse 1, introduces the song by declaring its purpose—to praise God for His triumph:

¹Then Moses and the children of Israel sang this song to the LORD, and spoke, saying:

'I will sing to the LORD,
For He has triumphed **gloriously**!
The horse and its rider
He has thrown into the sea!

In Hebrew, line 2 literally means, "He is gloriously glorious."[2] Lines 3 and 4 describe the triumph over the enemy.

Succeeding verses continue to describe and praise God, alternately emphasizing who God is and what He has done. In verses 2 and 3, Moses describes qualities of God, personal and national relationships with God, and God's role in this particular battle as "a man of war" (some versions, "warrior"):

²The LORD *is* my **strength** and **song**,
And He has become my **salvation**;
He *is* **my God**, and I will praise Him;
My father's God, and I will exalt Him.
³The LORD *is* a **man of war**;
The LORD *is* His name.

Terrified by the approaching army and trapped against the sea, the Israelites assumed they would die in the wilderness, so slavery seemed to be a better alternative. Though they outnumbered the Egyptians, the Israelites had no idea how to fight; they were clinging to the slave mentality of helpless dependence on their masters.

In contrast, God demonstrated His flawless character and power to deliver His people. Moses lists God's attributes:

- "strength" and "song," suggesting protection;

- "salvation," suggesting deliverance and rescue;

- "my God" and "my father's God," noting both a personal and generational relationship with God;

- "man of war," a warrior greater than any man or army who will fight for them.

Just Thinking . . .

1. How does God demonstrate these same attributes in the lives of Christians today?

2. Exodus 14:13-14 and 15:3 pictures God as a "warrior." Today, many prefer to emphasize God's love and compassion. Does God "fight" for His people (Christians) today? Does He expect us to "fight" against evil? Consider Romans 8:31-39 and Ephesians 6:11-13.

---

2   Walter C. Kaiser, Jr., "Exodus" in *Genesis, Exodus, Leviticus and Numbers,* The Expositor's Bible Commentary, ed. Frank E. Gaebelein, vol. 2 (Grand Rapids, Mich.: Zondervan, 1990) 394.

Notice the verbs as God takes action:

> [4]Pharaoh's chariots and his army He **has cast** into the sea;
> His chosen captains also **are drowned** in the Red Sea.
> [5]The depths **have covered** them;
> They **sank** to the bottom **like a stone.**

"Right hand" is often a reference to honor, power, and authority. Because He is powerful, God overcomes the enemy. Again, the verbs in the song evoke realistic images of the battle:

> [6]Your right hand, O LORD, has become glorious in power;
> Your right hand, O LORD, **has dashed the enemy in pieces.**
> [7]And in the greatness of Your excellence
> You **have overthrown** those who rose against You;
> You sent forth Your wrath;
> It **consumed** them like stubble.

God expressed His power through His own creation—wind and water—to overcome an arrogant enemy. Notice how the description of God's actions come before and after the enemy's prideful boasts, just as the wind and water and bed of the sea completely surrounded and overwhelmed the soldiers.

> [8]And with the **blast of Your nostrils**
> The waters were gathered together;
> The **floods stood upright** like a heap;
> The depths **congealed** in the heart of the sea.
>
> [9]The enemy said, 'I will pursue,
> I will overtake,
> I will divide the spoil;
> My desire shall be satisfied on them.
> I will draw my sword,
> My hand shall destroy them.'
>
> [10]You **blew with Your wind,**
> The sea covered them;
> They **sank like lead** in the mighty waters.

Verse 11 states that God's greatness and power are beyond compare; then verse 12 gives an example of that power in action.

> [11]Who *is* like You, O LORD, among the gods?
> Who *is* like You, glorious in holiness,
> Fearful in praises, doing wonders?
> [12]You stretched out Your right hand;
> The earth swallowed them.

"Earth swallowed them" might seem like a strange image because the sea actually swallowed the soldiers. However, the soldiers died and were buried in watery graves just as if they had been buried in the earth. In 1 Samuel 28:13, the woman who was told by King Saul to call up the spirit of Samuel saw "a spirit ascending out of the earth," that is, from a grave.[3] In another sense, all men are dust, and at death all return to the earth (Genesis 3:19).

3   Kaiser 395.

Stanza 2 begins with verse 13. Along with the victory over the army, Moses adds two more great works of God:

> ¹³You in Your mercy have **led** forth
> The people whom You have **redeemed;**
> You have **guided** *them* in Your strength
> To Your holy habitation.

God led them out of Egypt, redeeming them from slavery, and He will guide them to His "holy habitation." First they will go to Mt. Sinai and receive God's law, but ultimately, God will lead them to the Promised Land. "Holy habitation" probably refers to the temple on Mt. Zion (Deuteronomy 12:5, 11).[4] God is more than a warrior; He is their guide.

Just Thinking . . .

1. How did God lead, redeem, and guide the Israelites?

2. How does He lead, redeem, and guide us today?

The next verses anticipate conquering future enemies. Moses foresees how Philistia, Edom, Moab, and Canaan will react when they hear of God's power, strength, and mighty works (vv. 14-16; cf. Joshua 2:10-11). Verse 16 echoes the passage through the sea as well as their redemption (purchase).

> ¹⁴The people will hear *and* be afraid:
> **Sorrow** will take hold of the inhabitants of Philistia.
> ¹⁵Then the chiefs of Edom **will be dismayed;**
> The mighty men of Moab,
> **Trembling** will take hold of them;
> All the inhabitants of Canaan will **melt away.**
> ¹⁶**Fear and dread** will fall on them;
> By the greatness of Your arm
> They **will be** *as* **still as a stone,**
> Till Your people pass over, O Lᴏʀᴅ,
> Till the people pass over
> Whom You have purchased.

The next verses emphasize God's establishment of the people in the Promised Land:

> ¹⁷You will **bring** them in and **plant** them
> In the mountain of Your inheritance,
> *In* the place, O Lᴏʀᴅ, *which* You **have made**
> For Your own dwelling,
> The sanctuary, O Lᴏʀᴅ, *which* Your **hands have established.**

> ¹⁸The Lᴏʀᴅ **shall reign** forever and ever.

Verses 19-20 provide a narrative summation of the story, noting that Miriam, a prophetess and the sister of Aaron and Moses, led the women in playing timbrels and dancing. Verse 21 begins, "And Miriam answered them," basically repeating verse 1:

> ²¹'Sing to the Lᴏʀᴅ,
> For He has triumphed gloriously!

---

4   Kaiser 395.

The horse and its rider
He has thrown into the sea!'

Though we do not know exactly how the song was sung originally, this ending suggests that Miriam and the women repeated the first four lines of the song, like a chorus or responsive reading, perhaps after each major section.

Just Thinking . . .

1. Stanza 1 describes God's deliverance from the immediate danger of the Egyptian army (Exodus 15:1-12). Stanza 2 predicts God's guidance to the Promised Land (15:13-18). How does the first part reinforce the second part? What purposes are fulfilled by the song?

2. Divide the class into two groups. Let one group read in unison the Song of Moses and the other group respond with Miriam's song after verses 5, 10, 16, and 18. How does hearing the song affect the meaning, as opposed to reading it silently?

3. Read references to Miriam and discuss her personality and relationship with her brothers: Exodus 2:2, 7-8; Numbers 12:1-16; 20:1; Deuteronomy 24:8-10; Micah 6:3-5.

Application: Delivered to . . .

God delivered the Israelites *from* slavery, *from* an army of chariots, and *from* fear. The magnificent, awe-inspiring passage through the Red Sea provides a glimpse of God's creativity and power. Who but Jehovah God could ever think of such a remarkable, seemingly impossible feat, much less accomplish it?

Yet this great event was the means to a greater end. God had a plan that began with Joseph's suffering and triumph in Egypt and came to fruition when He established a covenant with His people at Mt. Sinai. Through Moses, God said,

'Now therefore, **if you will indeed obey My voice and keep My covenant, then you shall be a special treasure to Me above all people**; for all the earth *is* Mine. **And you shall be to Me a kingdom of priests and a holy nation**'(Exodus 19:5-6).

The Israelites were delivered *to* service for God. God's covenant with individuals like Abraham, Isaac, and Jacob grew into a relationship between God and the family of Jacob (Israel) and now with the entire nation, providing not only guidance and protection but also the Law that would unite and bind them to their God.

Having seen His power to deliver, the children of Israel committed themselves to God: "All that the LORD has spoken we will do." (Exodus 19:8)

We know that the Israelites often failed to keep their promise to God, yet He continued to work with and through them to accomplish His will. In Deuteronomy 18:15, Moses told the people, "The LORD your God will raise up for you a Prophet like me from your midst . . . Him you shall hear." In Acts 3:17-26, Peter proclaimed Jesus as the fulfillment of that prophecy, the One who would turn us from sin.

Today God still offers the opportunity for people to know and serve Him. Someone more glorious than Moses came to show us the way to God (Hebrews 3:1-3; John 14:6). His way is far more miraculous than the path through the Red Sea or the law God gave to Israel (John 1:17). As He delivered His people from slavery in Egypt, God is able to deliver us from sin through Jesus.

Just Thinking . . .

1. Deliverance continues as a theme throughout the Bible. Discuss these passages that express how God delivers His people from sin today: Romans 7:19-25; Colossians 1:9-14; 1 John 1:7.

2. Find a hymn that celebrates our deliverance from sin and sing it together.

Chapter 2
The Song of Deborah and Barak
Judges 5:1-31

Women Warriors of Israel

Beneath a palm tree between Ramah and Bethel, Deborah the prophetess and wife of Lapidoth held court, settling disputes among the Israelites. Here she listened to horror stories of Canaanite oppression, pondering Israel's sad condition and praying for deliverance. Would they never be free of enemies?

Deborah knew history; after Joshua and his generation died, the people turned to idol worship, so God allowed plunderers and pagans to conquer them. Under intolerable oppression, the people cried to the Lord, and He sent judges—warriors like Othniel, Ehud, and Shamgar—who vanquished their enemies and encouraged them to worship God once more.

Sadly, when the judge died, the people turned again to idols, which led to more oppression. For 20 years, Israel had cowered under the current tyrant, Jabin, a Canaanite king supported by Sisera and his army. No hero appeared; no man dared to challenge Jabin's 900 iron chariots. Only Deborah offered counsel and consolation, but she was no warrior.

Deborah felt certain that deliverance would come, but when? God had promised He would never desert His people, if they obeyed Him. If only she knew how God would deliver them . . . . Suddenly, Deborah did know. With confidence that only communication from God could produce, Deborah sent for a man named Barak, Abinoam's son, from Kedesh: "Tell him to hurry," she instructed the messenger. "God's word awaits him!"

* * *

Heber, a Kenite descended from Moses' father-in-law, sat outside his tent near the terebinth tree beside Kedesh. Despite ties with the Israelites, he avoided their conflicts. He also had ties with King Jabin of Hazor and had even welcomed Sisera to his tent. "Better to be at peace with all men," he thought. His wife Jael despised the Canaanites, especially Sisera, but what did a woman know of these things?

A passing Israelite spoke of troops from Naphtili and Zebulun gathering at Mt. Tabor. "Ridiculous," Heber said. "Who would dare challenge King Jabin?"

"They say Deborah, the judge near Ramah, told Barak to raise an army of 10,000 men." Could it be true? Then someone else told him that Barak and Deborah were marching to Kedesh.

Heber was astonished. "A woman, going into battle? They will be slaughtered!"

"Unless God is with them," another man chimed in. "They say Deborah thinks God will deliver Sisera into Barak's hands."

Troubled, Heber wondered if he should warn Sisera. He turned and found his wife Jael watching him. Had she heard the news? No matter. Heber needed to think. He left the camp.

Jael shivered and looked up at gathering clouds. A storm—from God? She knew Deborah to be wise and righteous, but a warrior? Amazing! Oh how Jael wished she could join the battle!

* * *

From Mt. Tabor, Barak and Deborah surveyed the valley below. Soon those dreadful iron chariots would be in sight, followed by numberless foot soldiers. How could Barak's ragtag, poorly armed troops hope to win?

Deborah sensed Barak's fear. When he heard God's command to attack Sisera, Barak had said, "I won't go unless you go with me." She agreed but warned him of the consequences: "There will be no glory for you, for the Lord will sell Sisera into the hand of a woman."

Now she encouraged him: "Has not the LORD gone out before you?"[5] Barak signaled his captains to move forward. As they left Mt. Tabor, thunder rumbled; rain fell.

Across the plains, Sisera admired the array of chariots, savoring his advantage until—thunder? This wasn't the rainy season. He urged his horses forward, hoping for a quick victory before the storm broke.

Hours later, after the Canaanites had abandoned their chariots to mud and flood waters, after the slaughter of many pagan soldiers, Barak stood over Sisera's dead body, flanked by Deborah and Jael. All that remained to be done was the writing of the song. (Based on Judges 4-5).

Just Thinking . . .

1. Deborah is the only woman judge. How do her roles as prophetess, wife, judge, and a mother in Israel contribute to the deliverance from Canaanite oppression?

2. Why do you think God chose a woman to participate in this deliverance?

The Song of Deborah and Barak

Deborah and Barak's victory is described twice, first as a narrative in Judges 4 and then as a song in Judges 5. Each version contributes details to create a complete report. The song begins in Judges 5:2 with an unbeatable combination for victory:

¹Then Deborah and Barak the son of Abinoam sang on that day, saying:

² 'When **leaders lead** in Israel,
When the **people willingly offer themselves,**
Bless the LORD!

³ 'Hear, O kings! Give ear, O princes!
I, *even* I, will sing to the LORD;
I will sing praise to the LORD God of Israel.

When leaders follow God's command and people willingly submit to that leadership, they all glorify God. This statement may be a gentle rebuke for Barak's reluctance to lead; then in verse 3, Deborah announces her praise of God to rulers everywhere, so all will know that the LORD won this battle. She is delighted to express this message of triumph and praise to God.

---

5   Herbert Wolf, "Judges" in *Deuteronomy, Joshua, Judges, Ruth, 1 and 2 Samuel,* The Expositor's Bible Commentary, ed. Frank E. Gaebelein, vol.3 (Grand Rapids, Mich.: Zondervan, 1992) 406. This phrase refers to a king marching ahead of his army. God was leading the attack.

Just Thinking . . .

1. Barak refuses to lead the army in battle unless Deborah goes with him. What does his request tell us about Deborah's character and reputation? (4:6-9,14).

2. What does it tell us about Barak?

Next, she compares God's participation in the battle with His appearance at Seir and Edom, names associated with Mt. Sinai, when thunder and lightning accompanied His meeting with the Israelites (Exodus 19:16).[6] Again God uses elements of His creation to overpower the enemies of Israel—thunder, rain, flood waters—all are at His command.

> [4] LORD, when You went out from Seir,
> When You marched from the field of Edom,
> The **earth trembled** and the **heavens poured,**
> The clouds also poured water;
> [5] The **mountains gushed** before the LORD,
> This Sinai, before the LORD God of Israel.

Verses 6-8 describe conditions prior to this battle. Shamgar, the hero who followed Ehud, is mentioned only here and in Judges 3:31; he "also delivered Israel" from the Philistines. After his death, conditions deteriorated in the present "days of Jael." Roads and villages were unsafe because of Canaanite oppression. The line about Deborah confirms her role as a judge who tried to stabilize daily life by administering the Law.

> [6] In the days of Shamgar, son of Anath,
> In the days of Jael,
> The highways were **deserted,**
> And the travelers walked along the byways.
> [7] **Village life ceased**, it ceased in Israel,
> Until I, Deborah, arose,
> Arose a mother in Israel.
> [8] They chose new gods;
> Then *there was* war in the gates;
> Not a shield or spear was seen among forty thousand in Israel.

Because the Israelites had chosen "new gods," war assaulted the city gates—a war of oppression, fear, and violence that further disrupted the economy and trade among the villages. Apparently, no warrior had appeared to lead the Israelites in battle until God chose Barak; the last line of verse 8 suggests the Israelites were either poorly armed or too afraid to fight.

By announcing God's commands to Barak, Deborah participated in rallying the troops and working with "the rulers of Israel." Notice that leaders and followers must be willing to "offer" themselves in God's service.

> [9] My heart *is* with the rulers of Israel
> Who offered themselves willingly with the people.
> Bless the LORD!
>
> [10] Speak, **you who ride on white donkeys,**
> Who sit in **judges' attire,**

6   Wolf 409.

And **who walk along the road.**
[11] Far from the noise of the archers, among the watering places,
There they shall recount the righteous acts of the Lord,
The righteous acts *for* His villagers in Israel;
Then the people of the Lord shall go down to the gates.

Verses 10 and 11 encourage "those who ride on white donkeys" (rich people) and "who sit in judges' attire" (rulers), "and who walk along the road" (all classes of people), to listen to the stories of the Lord's righteous acts.[7] Because of God's victory, people can safely conduct business at city gates. Peace has come to Israel.

Just Thinking . . .

1. Deborah delighted in telling the good news of victory and peace. Why were people from various levels of society willing to listen to her?

2. As Christians, how can we imitate her in our daily interactions with people? What "good news" can we share?

God called Barak to this battle; seeing him with captives reminds everyone of God's triumph. All who had survived the Canaanite oppression would know the Lord had fought for them.

[12] **Awake**, awake, Deborah!
Awake, awake, sing a song!
Arise, Barak, and lead your captives away,
O son of Abinoam!

[13] Then the survivors came down, the people against the nobles;
The Lord came down for me against the mighty.

Verses 14-18 offer praise for the tribes that sent men to fight and censure for the tribes that did not participate.

[14] From Ephraim *were* those whose roots were in Amalek.
After you, Benjamin, with your peoples,
From Machir rulers came down,
And from Zebulun those who bear the recruiter's staff.
[15] And the princes of Issachar *were* with Deborah;
As Issachar, so *was* Barak
Sent into the valley under his command;
Among the divisions of Reuben
There were great resolves of heart.
[16] **Why did you sit among the sheepfolds,**
To hear the pipings for the flocks?
The divisions of Reuben have great searchings of heart.
[17] Gilead stayed beyond the Jordan,
And why did Dan remain on ships?
Asher continued at the seashore,
And stayed by his inlets.
[18] Zebulun *is* a people *who* jeopardized their lives to the point of death,
Naphtali also, on the heights of the battlefield.

---

7   Wolf 411.

These verses add information not included in the narrative. Though the main army came from Naphtali and Zebulun, Barak apparently recruited soldiers from the other tribes, but some refused. Deborah shames those who stayed in their sheepfolds and ships while their brothers risked their lives.

In verse 19, Deborah remembers that Canaanite kings had often plundered Israelite cities and villages. This time, however, they took no spoils.

> ¹⁹ The kings came *and* fought,
> Then the kings of Canaan fought
> In Taanach, by the waters of Megiddo;
> They took no spoils of silver.
> ²⁰ They fought from the heavens;
> The **stars** from their courses fought against Sisera.
> ²¹ The **torrent of Kishon** swept them away,
> That ancient torrent, the torrent of Kishon.
> O my soul, march on in strength!
> ²² Then the horses' hooves pounded,
> The galloping, galloping of his steeds.
> ²³ 'Curse Meroz,' said the angel of the LORD,
> 'Curse its inhabitants bitterly,
> **Because they did not come to the help of the LORD,**
> To the help of the LORD against the mighty.'

Notice the repetition of "fought" and "river" and references to "stars" and "heavens" fighting Sisera; these are metaphors for God and His use of natural forces (rain and floods) to disrupt the Canaanite army at the Kishon River.[8] Deborah seems overwhelmed with God's magnificent triumph. However, she also notes that God curses Meroz, a city that suffered from Canaanite oppression but did not join Barak in battle, for failing "to help the LORD" (v. 23).

Just Thinking . . .

1. Some tribes joined Barak in battle; others did not. What does this reaction tell us about the organization and government of Israel during the period of the judges?

2. Did God need the "help" of all the tribes to win the battle? If not, why did it matter if some failed to join Barak and Deborah?

Verses 24-27 recount Jael's victory over Sisera in gruesome detail. For a soldier to be killed by a woman was humiliating. Deborah's lavish praise for Jael creates contrasts: Barak hesitated before the battle; Sisera ran away when his chariots become useless; Jael, however, demonstrated cunning and courage when she killed a hated pagan enemy.

> ²⁴ "Most **blessed among women** is Jael,
> The wife of Heber the Kenite;
> Blessed is she among women in tents.
>
> ²⁵ He asked for water, she gave milk;
> She brought out cream in a lordly bowl.
> ²⁶ She **stretched her hand** to the tent peg,
> Her right hand to the workmen's hammer;

---

8   Wolf 414.

She **pounded** Sisera, she pierced his head,

She **split and struck** through his temple.
²⁷ At her feet he **sank**, he **fell**, he **lay still;**
At her feet he sank, he fell;
Where he sank, there he fell dead.

The verbs in these verses create a vivid image of treachery and triumph. First Jael welcomed and served Sisera, making him feel safe. When he fell asleep, she "pounded" Sisera, "pierced his head," and "split and struck through his temple."⁹

Three times in verse 27, we read that Sisera "sank" and "fell" at Jael's feet. Judges 4:17-21 reveals that Sisera was already reclining, so Deborah probably refers to his defeat rather than his physical position when he was struck. Repetition highlights the drama—a mighty warrior dying not in battle but in shameful humiliation at a woman's feet.

Deborah obviously approves of Jael's actions, calling her "most blessed among women" (5:24). While we may cringe at the violence, we should remember that Jael receives the credit for delivering Israel from an infamous barbarian who had served a pagan king in harsh oppression of Israel for 20 years. She is exalted for her courage.

Just Thinking . . .

1. Why did Sisera trust Jael?

2. How can we reconcile her treachery with her heroism?

3. How does Jael compare in bravery with Barak, Sisera, and Deborah?

Deborah moves from the image of Sisera dead at Jael's feet to an image of his mother, looking through a window. Perhaps remembering how many Israelite mothers had waited in vain for their sons to return from other battles, Deborah imagines Sisera's mother waiting for him, wondering at his delay (v. 28).

²⁸ The mother of Sisera looked through the window,
And cried out through the lattice,
'Why is his chariot *so* long in coming?
Why tarries the clatter of his chariots?'
²⁹ Her wisest ladies answered her,
Yes, she answered herself,

³⁰ 'Are they not finding and dividing the spoil:
To every man a girl *or* two;
For Sisera, plunder of dyed garments,
Plunder of garments embroidered and dyed,
Two pieces of dyed embroidery for the neck of the looter?'

³¹ Thus let all Your enemies perish, O Lord!
But *let* those who love Him *be* like the sun
When it comes out in full strength.

---

9 Wolf 407. If we wonder how a woman had the strength to pierce Sisera's head, we should understand that women of that time usually put up and took down the tents. Jael was strong and skilled with tools.

Those who wait for loved ones to return from war suffer great anxiety. Friends of Sisera's mother offer support by describing how soldiers who are busy claiming the spoils of war don't think of those who wait at home. Though verses 28-30 may sound smug or vengeful, they also provide a poignant reminder that war causes suffering for everyone.

Verse 31 ends the song with two requests: may all the LORD's enemies perish like Sisera, and may all who love God be "like the sun . . . in full strength" After the song, a single narrative sentence notes that "the land had rest for forty years," suggesting that Deborah continued as judge for that time period (cf. Judges 2:18- 19).

Just Thinking . . .

1. Who is the real hero celebrated in the Song of Deborah? How does this song compare with the Song of Moses and Miriam?

2. As Christians, what lessons from this song apply to us today?

3. What can we learn from the Israelites' disobedience and repentance? How can we avoid the mistakes they made?

Application: What Went Wrong?

Like the Song of Moses, the Song of Deborah served as a reminder of God's power and concern for His people. God delivered the Israelites *from* Jabin and Sisera so He could deliver them *to* obedience and the blessings of His covenant relationship. Sadly, the Book of Judges continues with the saga of cyclical disobedience and deliverance.

What led the entire nation into disobedience time after time? Why would they forsake God and worship idols after promising Joshua they would serve only the LORD? Judges 2:10 tells us: ". . . another generation arose after them who did not know the LORD nor the work which He had done for Israel."

The generation that promised to serve God did not teach their children to serve God. They failed to follow specific instructions to put God first and to teach their children diligently and daily, by words and deeds (Deuteronomy 6:4-9). God even told them to "beware, lest you forget the LORD . . . fear the LORD your God and serve Him . . .You shall not go after other gods, the gods of the peoples who are all around you . . . " (6:12-14).

Failure to teach in the home led to a shortage of godly leaders. Judges 21:25 tells us, "In those days there was no king in Israel; everyone did what was right in his own eyes." Without a king, Israel had prospered by depending on God and the leaders He chose. Moses and Joshua were names synonymous with faithful obedience, but successive generations knew less about these heroes, and the judges didn't unify the tribes. Lacking leaders who would hold them accountable to God, each person lived selfishly, following his or her own moral code. Perhaps you have heard today's version of this attitude: "What's right for you isn't right for me; I must follow my heart."

As Christians, we should learn at least three lessons from Deborah and her song:

- **We must** teach our children foundational Christianity—know and love God; follow Christ; obey the inspired word; live by faith (Genesis 1:1; John 1:1; Mark 12:29-31; John 14:6; Acts 4:12; 2 Timothy 3:16-17; 2 Corinthians 5:7; Hebrews 11:6).

- **We must** teach by example, living our faith, so our children will know how to live their faith and how to lead others to Christ (Ephesians 6:1-2; 1 Timothy 4:12; 2 Timothy 2:2; Matthew 28:18-20).

- **We must** remember that God can use even one faithful person; others will follow a faithful leader. With God's help, good leaders grow from good teaching.

Chapter 3
The Song of Hannah
1 Samuel 2:1-10

A Mother's Vow

"I am barren," Hannah whispered. The words lay like stones on her heart, but she couldn't deny the truth. Early in her marriage to Elkanah, she thought, "Soon we'll have a baby; I must be patient." As months turned into years, she prayed more often, desperately seeking the reason for God's displeasure. When Elkanah took Peninnah as his second wife, Hannah wept, but she understood. "A man must have sons," she thought. She tried to set aside her pain.

Then Peninnah had a baby—and another. Her husband was happy, and Hannah tried to accept what she could not change. Seeing Hannah's distress, Peninnah provoked her with sly remarks about taking care of babies or comments on Elkanah's pride in his children.

Each barb drew heart's blood, and old scars didn't protect her from new wounds. The worst times were the annual trips to Shiloh for worship, and tonight was no different. Elkanah returned from the tabernacle with portions of meat from the sacrifice. Peninnah and the children laughed and celebrated, but the double portion for Hannah only emphasized her sad condition. She couldn't eat, and when Elkanah saw her tears, he tried to comfort her. "Am I not better to you than ten sons?"

Hannah turned away. He meant well; he didn't blame her or love her less because she was barren, but nothing could compensate for what she couldn't have. To Hannah, the highest act of love was to give her husband a son, and she had failed. She left the family circle to seek consolation in prayer.

In the tabernacle, she fell face down. What new words could she say? Her lips moved soundlessly; in bitterness of soul and anguished tears, she prayed. Then she vowed, "O LORD of hosts, if You will indeed look on the affliction of Your maidservant and remember me, and not forget Your maidservant, but will give Your maidservant a male child, then I will give him to the LORD all the days of his life, and no razor shall come upon his head."[10]

She didn't notice Eli the priest until she heard his harsh words. "How long will you be drunk?"

Startled, Hannah quickly explained, "I am a woman of sorrowful spirit; I have poured out my soul before the LORD." Realizing his mistake, Eli blessed Hannah, and she returned to Elkanah, no longer sad.

In due time, she had a son, Samuel, "Because I have asked for him from the LORD." When she had weaned him, she and Elkanah took the young child to Eli and left him to become a priest, prophet, judge, and faithful servant to God and Israel. Then Hannah expressed her joy in song. (Based on 1 Samuel 1).

---

10   Ronald F. Youngblood, "1 and 2 Samuel" in *Deuteronomy, Joshua, Judges, Ruth, 1 and 2 Samuel*, The Expositor's Bible Commentary, ed. Frank E. Gaebelein, vol.3 (Grand Rapids, Mich.: Zondervan, 1992) 573. Youngblood notes that "remember me" doesn't mean God is forgetful; it is Hannah's way of asking for special attention or care.

1. Read 1 Samuel 1. How did Hannah's barrenness affect her husband and Peninnah as well as herself?

2. Who did Hannah blame for her condition?

Hannah's Song

The Bible says that Hannah prayed, but her utterance has the lyrical qualities of a song of victory and joy, giving all the glory to God. Scholars suggest her prayer may have been a favorite song memorized from the tabernacle worship, partly because of references to weapons and to God's power against adversaries (1 Samuel 2:3,10). In addition, David echoes Hannah's imagery in 2 Samuel 22:2-51, showing that certain phrases were used consistently in songs of different time periods.[11] However, other references seem personal.

Original or not, the song beautifully expresses love, joy, and confidence in God's great power. Hannah never says, "Thank You for giving me a son." Instead, she exalts God's immense power and concern. She also realizes that God's deliverance extends beyond her personal desire and points to greater deliverance for Israel and the world.

The verbs in verse 1 clearly set the tone for the song.

> [1]My heart **rejoices** in the LORD;
> My horn **is exalted** in the LORD.
> I **smile** at my enemies,
> Because I **rejoice** in Your salvation.

"My horn" symbolizes strength, a reference to deer, oxen and other animals that use their antlers or horns as weapons. Hannah's strength has been increased "in the LORD."[12] She is no longer a victim of harassment. She finds joy in the LORD's salvation or deliverance from her barren state.

> [2]No one is **holy** like the LORD,
> For *there is* **none besides You,**
> Nor *is there* any **rock** like our God.

Verse 2 identifies three qualities of God: holiness, uniqueness, and rock-like strength. The image of the rock also suggests refuge and is found frequently in the Psalms (Psalms 18, 42, 62, and 71, among others). Hannah praises God not only for what He has done but also for Who He is—the incomparable One.

> [3]**Talk** no more so **very proudly;**
> Let no **arrogance** come from **your mouth,**
> For the LORD *is* the God of knowledge;
> And by Him **actions are weighed.**

Verse 3 moves from God's qualities to human qualities, specifically pride. Notice the parallel structure that emphasizes the same idea twice: "talk/from your mouth" and "so very proudly/arrogance." This warning applies to everyone, suggesting that in comparison with God's great power and mighty works, people have no reason to be arrogant and proud. However, it may also refer specifically to Peninnah.

---

11   Youngblood 578-579.
12   Youngblood 580.

Just Thinking . . .

1. Why did Peninnah "provoke" Hannah?

2. How do you think she felt when she learned Hannah was pregnant? When Samuel was born and given to Eli? When Hannah had other children?

In verses 4-8, Hannah lists seven contrasting examples of how God uses His power among His people, often in surprising ways.

> [4] The **bows** of the mighty men *are* **broken,**
> And those who stumbled are girded with **strength.**
> [5] *Those who were* **full** have **hired themselves out for bread,**
> And the **hungry** have **ceased** *to hunger.*
> Even the **barren** has **borne seven,**
> And she who has many children has become **feeble.**
>
> [6] The LORD kills and makes alive;
> He brings down to the grave and brings up.
>
> [7] The LORD makes **poor** and makes **rich;**
> He brings **low** and **lifts up.**
> [8] He **raises the poor** from the dust
> *And* **lifts the beggar** from the ash heap,
> To set *them* among princes
> And make them inherit the throne of glory.
>
> For the pillars of the earth *are* the LORD's,
> And He has set the world upon them.

The first contrast is strong verses weak; God can break the weapons (bows) of "mighty men," disabling those who appear to be strong. At the same time, He "girded with strength" those who are weak. Battlefield language in verse 4 suggests the many times that God led His people to victory over stronger foes. Centuries later, the writer of Hebrews would echo this contrast for Jewish Christians with examples of the strong made weak and the weak made strong (Hebrews 11:32-34).

Verse 5 has two contrasts: full verses hungry and barren verses fertile. Those who customarily have plenty to eat may suddenly find themselves in want, but God provides food for the hungry. When she sings of the barren who "has borne seven," Hannah probably exaggerates to emphasize God's ability to reverse a woman's barrenness and make her fertile. Seven could just mean "many," but it is often used to represent perfection or completeness in the Old Testament, so a woman who had seven children after being barren would have achieved a high status.

In 1 Samuel 2:19-21, we learn that Hannah and Elkanah visited Samuel each year and received Eli's blessing so that Hannah had five more children! The contrast of "she who has many children has become feeble" could also be a reference to Peninnah in the sense that she had lost her power to provoke Hannah.

Verse 6 contrasts God's power over death and life as well as sickness and health: "The LORD kills and makes alive; He brings down to the grave and brings up." Because God IS God, because He created mankind, He has the ultimate right to give life and take it, to allow sickness or danger and to heal or rescue those afflicted. He does not exercise this power lightly; He follows His divine nature and purpose.

The Bible contains numerous examples of God's sovereign power such as the Flood and the plagues in Egypt, and Hannah's brief statement here captures what should have been well-known among the Israelites because of verses like Deuteronomy 32:39: 'Now see that I, *even* I, *am* He, And *there is* no God besides Me; I kill and I make alive; I wound and I heal; Nor *is there any* who can deliver from My hand."

The second line of verse 6 may suggest resurrection, but it probably refers more to life-threatening illness or danger contrasted with rescue from death. For instance, Isaac was only inches from death at the hand of Abraham when God intervened (Genesis 22:7-13). Later examples include David in Psalm 30, Hezekiah in 2 Kings 20, and Jonah.

Verse 7 contrasts the poor and the rich as well as the lowly and the exalted. Verse 8 repeats these examples with more vivid imagery. A poor man might live in dust; a lowly beggar might mourn on the ash heap, but by God's power, poor men can rise to riches and positions of honor (Job 2:8; 42:10). Psalm 113 echoes these lines and includes a verse about a barren woman made to be "a joyful mother of children."[13] Hannah's contrasts represent descriptions of God found throughout the Old Testament. At the end of verse 8, she explains why God exerts control in these areas: "For the pillars of the earth are the Lord's, And He has set the world upon them."

Just Thinking . . .

1. How does God work among His people today in light of the seven contrasts Hannah describes?

2. Compare the last two lines of verse 8 with Job 38:4-6. We might summarize the two passages this way: "What God made, He ultimately rules." Do people today understand that God has dominion over the world because He made it? Why or why not?

The Hebrew word translated "saints" in verse 9 means "one to whom the Lord has pledged his covenant love," which is the opposite of "the wicked."[14] God will guard His saints wherever they go, protecting them from the wicked who cannot prevail by mere human strength.

> [9] He will **guard** the feet of His **saints,**
> But the **wicked** shall be **silent** in darkness.
> For by strength no man shall prevail.
> [10] The **adversaries** of the Lord shall be **broken in pieces;**
> From heaven He will **thunder against them.**
> The Lord will **judge** the ends of the earth.
>
> He will **give strength** to His king,
> And **exalt the horn** of His anointed.

Verse 10 takes us back to verse 3 with the imagery of breaking enemies into pieces as He broke the bows of the strong men. God will "thunder against them," a phrase that suggests troubling or provoking, which might be another comment on Peninnah who provoked Hannah as a rival.[15]

Finally, Hannah notes the Lord's role as judge and as the provider of strength to His king. He will also "exalt the horn [strength] of His anointed." Israel did not have a king at this time, but the idea of an anointed or God-chosen leader was deeply rooted in Israelite history—Moses predicted that God would raise up "a Prophet

---

13   Youngblood 581.

14   Youngblood 581.

15   Youngblood 572, 581.

28

like me" (Deuteronomy 18:15)—and various judges chosen (anointed) by God had ruled the people for years. Eli was out of favor because his sons were corrupt (1 Samuel 3:12-17); Samuel would be the last judge and the one to anoint the first two kings, Saul and David. Ultimately, David's descendant would rule forever as Messiah, God's Anointed.

Just Thinking . . .

1. The second line of verse 10 mentions that God will "thunder" against His enemies. How does this line echo thoughts from the songs of Moses and Deborah? Compare it also with Hebrews 11:32-34.

2. The last two lines of verse 10 prophesy about judgment and a King whom God will exalt. Compare with 2 Samuel 22:51, Psalm 96:13, and Matthew 28:18. Who is the King?

Hannah's Path to Deliverance

God delivered Hannah *from* the stigma of barrenness and the constant nettling of Peninnah, *from* the sorrow of an empty womb and empty arms, and *from* the self-imposed guilt of imagined sin. His deliverance was sure and complete but slow in coming. Based on the statement that Elkanah gave portions of meat "to Peninnah his wife and to all her sons and daughters" (1 Samuel 1:4), we can assume Hannah suffered with the burden of barrenness for years.

How did she move from the helpless state of despair to the dramatic and remarkable decision to ask God for a son whom she would give back to God? How could she sacrifice what she had wanted more than anything or anyone else in the world for so long?

Is it possible that Hannah's suffering prepared her for sacrifice?

Hannah's desire for a son to please her husband or heal her wounded pride or triumph over Peninnah had been honed to a sharpness of higher purpose by years of suffering. Her vow resulted not from suddenly guessing what would "make" God give her what she wanted, but from the realization that she could be blessed to give God something—someone—valuable. Binding Samuel to service in the tabernacle provided Israel with a great priest, prophet, judge, and servant who would unify the nation, draw them back to God from idolatry, and put in place King David, the ancestor of the Messiah and hope of the whole world.

Suffering taught Hannah to love God more than she loved anyone else—husband, child, or self. God delivered Hannah *to* keeping her vow and *to* sacrificing the maternal joy of watching her child grow up. Consequently, God also delivered her *to* greater earthly joy—five more children—as well as *to* greater knowledge of God and deeper joy in worshiping Him. No wonder her song is so joyous!

Nobody likes to suffer. We often hear people say that they can't or won't believe in God because He allows human suffering. Yet the Bible shows us repeatedly that suffering may draw us closer to God. Suffering is the crucible of faith, endurable because "we know that all things work together for good to those who love God, to those who are the called according to *His* purpose" (Romans 8:28), even if we don't live to see that good accomplished.

Application: What about Our Children?

There is a sense in which all godly parents should vow to rear their children to serve God. Among the Jews, every firstborn son belonged to God and was symbolically dedicated with an animal sacrifice (Exodus 13:2). Thus Mary and Joseph took Baby Jesus to the temple and offered two doves or pigeons (Luke 2:22-24).

Our children are precious gifts from God. We are not told to offer then to God in a tabernacle or on a cross, but we are told to bring them up "in the training and admonition of the Lord" (Ephesians 6:4). Yet recent studies tell us that many young people leave the church when they leave home; many more practice only a surface religion.

How far and fast would Christianity spread if we gave our children to God in the spirit of Hannah? How faithful would our children be if they heard God's word read daily in their homes and saw it practiced fully by their parents? Hannah loved Samuel. It was hard to leave her little son with Eli, but she knew she was also leaving him with God, and the God Hannah described in her song was surely capable of taking care of Samuel.

We want the best for our children—education, good jobs, happy homes. Hannah devoted her son to serving God. If we teach our children to love God and live for Him, will He not provide the best life for them? (Matthew 6:33).

Just Thinking . . .

1. Remembering how desperately Hannah wanted a son, how do you think she was able to fulfill her vow and give Samuel to God?

2. List the ways that God delivered Hannah. In what ways should we imitate her?

Chapter 4
The Song of David
2 Samuel 22:1-20, Part 1

Looking at the Heart

Hannah's son Samuel, the last judge of Israel, poured oil on the head of David, a handsome young shepherd. His bright eyes met the old priest's steady gaze with wonder. *Anointed of God! King of Israel! How could this be?*

Samuel had similar thoughts. God had sent him to Bethlehem to find a king among Jesse's sons. The oldest, Eliab, was tall and stately, but God surprised Samuel: "Don't look at his height or appearance; look at his heart, as I do." Jesse presented seven sons; seven times, God said, "No."

Samuel asked, "Do you have other sons?"

"Only the youngest; he keeps the sheep."

When David arrived, God said, "Anoint him." Satisfied that God's Spirit now rested on His chosen one, Samuel went home, leaving David to contemplate his new role.

The young shepherd must have struggled to sort out his feelings. *How can I be the king of Israel? My lord Saul is the king—a hero, a mighty warrior—I would never dare to challenge the Lord's anointed! Yet Samuel, the great prophet and judge, said God has chosen a new king.*

Because he couldn't comprehend how or when this business would be accomplished, he decided to wait upon the LORD. He went back to tend the sheep.

Near Gibeah, King Saul's servants struggled with a different problem. Since God's Spirit had departed from Saul because of his disobedience, the king was subject to fits of temper and distress that bordered on madness. Someone suggested that music might calm him; one bold servant approached the king: "I have seen a young man from Bethlehem, a son of Jesse. He plays skillfully, and he is a mighty man of war, prudent, and handsome. And the LORD is with him."

Perhaps Saul found that last quality most appealing; he missed God. So he sent for David, whose songs refreshed him, and David loved Saul. He traveled back and forth between his home and Saul's, content with the honor of service.

Time passed. One day when he returned to Saul's camp after a lengthy absence, David found the army arrayed for battle against the Philistines, yet no one gave the order to attack. As he talked with his brothers who served in Saul's army, a huge Philistine stepped forward and issued an amazing challenge. Goliath of Gath, more than nine feet tall, shouted, "I defy the armies of Israel. Send one man to fight me; if he kills me, we will be your servants. But if I kill him, you will be our servants."

David thought, "There will be a great reward for the man who kills this giant." He looked around expectantly; who would go? But no one volunteered. The Israelite soldiers looked at their shoes.

"He has challenged us for 40 days," someone muttered.

David realized they were all terrified. He cried out, "Who is this uncircumcised Philistine who defies the armies of the living God?"

In angry shame, his brothers told him to go home to the sheep pens, but David continued to ask questions. When Saul heard the ruckus and sent for him, David boldly said, "Your servant will fight this Philistine."

Saul protested, "You are a youth; he is a seasoned warrior."

"I've fought a lion and a bear," said David. "The LORD, who delivered me from the paw of the lion and the bear, He will deliver me from the hand of this Philistine."

Perhaps Saul recalled his early days as king, when he feared no one because he knew God was with him. Perhaps he recognized his own former confidence, long since lost, firmly established in this brave young solider. "Go with God," he said.

Refusing Saul's ill-fitting armor, David gathered five stones and gripped his sling as he turned to face the giant. Goliath arrogantly taunted the youth: "Am I dog? Will you fight me with sticks? I'll feed your flesh to the birds and the beasts!"

"You come with a sword, a spear, and a javelin," called David. "I come in the name of the LORD of hosts, the God of Israel whom you defy. This day the LORD will deliver you into my hand; I will strike you and take your head. I will give the Philistines to the birds and the beasts, that all the earth may know that there is a God in Israel; the battle is the LORD's!"

David ran toward Goliath, striking him in the forehead with one stone. The giant fell face down; the ground shook. David grabbed Goliath's sword and severed his head. Behind him, he heard a shout that echoed through the valley as Israel's army lost all fear and pursued the Philistines all the way to Gath and Ekron. (Based on 1 Samuel 16-17).

Just Thinking . . .

1. Read 1 Samuel 16-17. Why do you think David was willing to accept Goliath's challenge when no one else would?

2. What qualities does David have that suggest he will be a good king?

David the Psalmist

Moses, Miriam, Deborah, Barak, Hannah, and other men and women contributed songs to the Bible, but David, whose rise to fame and power began publically when he killed Goliath, wrote dozens of songs and prayers that still speak to millions today. Of the 150 poems included in the Bible's Book of Psalms, 73 are by or about David, but not one mentions Goliath. Yet within this remarkable event recorded in 1 Samuel 17, we find the theme that is woven like a golden thread through David's life: God's deliverance.

When David spoke of killing a lion and a bear, the word he used suggests that he "snatched" the lamb from the animal's mouth, preserving its life and then killing the predator.[16] He credited the LORD with delivering or rescuing him *from* wild animals, and he knew "this uncircumcised Philistine will be like one of them" (17:36). Having experienced God's physical rescue at least twice, he expected God to surrender Goliath into his hand as he snatched the honor of the LORD and Israel from this prideful pagan.

---

16   *Strong's Concordance with Hebrew and Greek Lexicon* online: "natsal" # 5337. www.eliyah.com/lexicon. html

David's Life and Influence

Like all writers of the Bible, David wrote by inspiration of the Holy Spirit. His psalms not only reveal knowledge of God's character and nature but also expand our understanding of David's life, especially regarding the depth and intimacy of his relationship with God.

For instance, Psalm 23 tells us that David trusted God and depended on Him as a sheep depends on the shepherd—an appropriate connection for a shepherd boy who led his nation and became the ancestor of the Good Shepherd.

Then we have Psalm 8, which could have influenced Paul's writing: "For since the creation of the world His invisible attributes are clearly seen, being understood by the things that are made, even His eternal power and Godhead . . . " (Romans 1:20). David celebrated God's creation.

Though we haven't killed a giant or led an army, we find ourselves—our hopes and fears, joys and sorrows—in the psalms. Writing and collecting the Book of Psalms may be David's best gift to posterity (2 Samuel 23:1-2).

Just Thinking . . .

1. Find three psalms attributed to David and write down phrases that are similar to the song from 2 Samuel 22.

2. Find two psalms attributed to other writers such as Asaph or the sons of Korah. How do they compare with David's psalms? How are they different?

Seeking Deliverance

Modern scholars list seven categories of songs in the Book of Psalms: Hymns, Laments, Thanksgiving, Remembrance, Confidence, Wisdom, and Royal.[17] Of course, subjects overlap; hymns may contain thanksgiving or a lament may ask for help and offer praise for past help. Songs of deliverance don't constitute a separate category, and not every psalm of David fits that description. However, he often sought God's guidance and depended on God to answer his request. "You are my hiding place; You shall preserve me from trouble; You shall surround me with songs of deliverance" (Psalm 32:7).

Representative of David's writing that celebrates God's deliverance is a formal, extended song of deliverance that offers thanks to God for his royal accomplishments. It appears twice in Scripture, as Psalm 18 in the Book of Psalms and as the Song of David in 2 Samuel 22. There are slight differences in the two versions, and we don't know which was written first. For instance, Psalm 18 begins, "I will love You, O Lord, my strength," but the version in 1 Samuel 22 omits this sentence.

Perhaps David first wrote the song as personal praise for God and later edited it for use as a national song of praise and thanksgiving. Both versions state that David composed this song "on the day when the Lord had delivered him from the hand of all his enemies, and from the hand of Saul" (Heading, Psalm 18; 2 Samuel 22:1). We should remember that events in 1 and 2 Samuel are not always presented in chronological order. While the song comes near the end of this history of David, it was not written at the end of his life.

Instead, it was probably written at the peak of his career, after he was well established as the king of Israel and Judah, when "the Lord had given him rest from all his enemies all around" (2 Samuel 7:1).

---

17   Eddie Cloer, *Psalms 1-50,* Truth for Today Commentary, ed. Eddie Cloer, (Searcy, Ar.: Resource Publications, 2005) 23-24.

In 2 Samuel 8, we find a list of the kings David had conquered who now paid tribute to him. During this time of peace, David wanted to build a "house" for God, but God tells him that David's son would build it.

More importantly, God made a covenant with David, stating that his throne would be established forever (v. 16). Furthermore, because of the song's joyful tone, the song must have been written before David's sins of adultery and murder. Consider this comment about the tone of the Song of David:

> But there is no trace in it [the Song] of the sorrow and shame that clouded over his [David's] later days; and no man whose conscience was stained with sins so dark as those of adultery and murder could have written words so strongly asserting his integrity and the cleanness of his hands as are found in verses 21-25. The psalm belongs to David's happiest time, when he had won for Israel security and empire. It is written from first to last in a tone of jubilant exultation . . . .[18]

In this chapter and the next one, we will review the song's introduction, three main setions, and conclusion.[19]

The Song of David, Introduction and Part 1

(2 Samuel 22:1-20)

The heading, mentioned earlier, is in verse 1; verses 2-4 introduce the song's subject:

> [2]The LORD *is* my **rock** and my **fortress** and my **deliverer;**
> [3] The God of my **strength**, in whom I will trust;
> My **shield** and the **horn of my salvation,**
> My **stronghold** and my **refuge;**
> My **Savior**, You save me from violence.
> [4] I will call upon the LORD, *who is worthy* **to be praised;**
> So shall I be saved from my enemies.

Nine nouns illustrate characteristics of the LORD; seven of them emphasize His power and strength. As in Hannah's song, "horn" symbolizes strength, so "horn of my salvation" intensifies the word "strength" in the previous line and stresses the certainty of God's saving power. "Rock," "fortress," "stronghold," and "refuge" suggest military strength and solid places of protection or shelter. "Shield" implies defense or protection.

"Deliverer" and "Savior" focus on God as a divine Person ready to save those who trust Him. The possessive pronoun "my" emphasizes David's personal relationship with God. Though not of the earth, God is close to David; though Spirit, God understands David's human needs. Several of these nine words occur in other psalms (Psalms 19:14; 31:3; 40:17; 42:9; 70:5; 71:3; 91:2; 144:1-2).

Verse 4 emphasizes God's worthiness and states confidently that the LORD will save when David calls on Him.

---

18   R. Payne Smith, "2 Samuel" in *Ruth, 1 Samuel, and 2 Samuel,* The Pulpit Commentary, ed. H.D.M. Spence and Joseph S. Exell, vol.4, (Grand Rapids, Mich.: Wm. B. Eerdmans Publishing Co., 1950) 530.
19   Youngblood 1065.

Just Thinking . . .

1. What do the nine nouns in verses 3-4 tell us about God's character?

2. Think of a time in your life when you found strength and hope in knowing these characteristics of God.

Verses 5-7 focus on God's deliverance of David from death:

> [5] When the **waves** of death surrounded me,
> The **floods** of ungodliness made me afraid.
> [6] The **sorrows** of Sheol surrounded me;
> The **snares** of death confronted me.
>
> [7] In my **distress** I called upon the LORD,
> And **cried** out to my God;
> He **heard** my voice from His temple,
> And my cry *entered* His ears.

David captures the feelings of being surrounded by threats of death—waves, floods, and the sorrows of Sheol, the unseen place of the dead. He pictures death as a hunter who sets snares or traps for the unsuspecting prey. David remembers situations when he expected to die. Twice Saul threw a spear at David and relentlessly pursued him through the wilderness. No doubt David also faced many enemies as he fought to secure Israel's borders.

Whenever he was in distress of death, he "cried" to God in His temple, and God heard him. "Temple" probably refers to heaven since the earthly temple had not yet been built.

Verses 8-16 form a theophany or description of God demonstrating His presence through natural events such as earthquakes and storms.[20]

> [8] Then the earth shook and trembled;
> The **foundations of heaven** quaked and were shaken,
> Because He was angry.
> [9] Smoke went up from His nostrils,
> And devouring **fire** from His mouth;
> Coals were kindled by it.
> [10] He bowed the heavens also, and came down
> With **darkness** under His feet.
> [11] He rode upon a **cherub**, and flew;
> And He was seen upon the **wings of the wind.**
> [12] He made **darkness canopies** around Him,
> Dark waters *and* thick **clouds** of the skies.
> [13] From the brightness before Him
> **Coals of fire** were kindled.
>
> [14] The LORD **thundered** from heaven,
> And the Most High **uttered His voice.**

---

20   Youngblood 1068.

¹⁵ He sent out **arrows** and scattered them;
Lightning bolts, and He vanquished them.
¹⁶ Then the channels of the sea were seen,
The **foundations of the world** were uncovered,

At the **rebuke** of the Lord,
At the **blast** of the breath of His nostrils.

Verse 8 describes God's answer to David's cry—anger expressed in massive activity of the elements in heaven and on the earth. The very foundations of heaven "quaked and were shaken." David describes the wrath of God as He "came down" with smoke and fire so hot that "coals were kindled by it," with darkness and clouds that conceal Him, with a cherub and "wings of the wind that" carry Him, and then His brightness.

The Lord also "thundered" and "uttered His voice." God's "rebuke" with "lightning flashes" routed the enemies. Verse 16 balances "foundations of the world" with "foundations of heaven" in verse 8; God has complete dominion over heaven and earth.

The language of this section echoes descriptions by Moses and Deborah and previews similar descriptions by prophets later on (Exodus 19:16-20; Judges 5:4-5; Isaiah 6:1-8; Habakkuk 3:3-15). In addition, references to sea channels and foundations of the world relate to Genesis 1:6-10, when God established the boundaries of sea and land during Creation.

Consider also John 12:27-33 for a similar example of God expressing Himself through nature. When Jesus described His death and said, "Father, glorify Your name," a voice from heaven confirmed His words, but some of those present thought they heard thunder. Bright light, an overshadowing cloud, and a voice from the cloud also occurred at the Transfiguration of Jesus (Matthew 17:1-8; Mark 9:2-7).

While such a display of dramatic activity in nature may seem strange to modern people with scientific knowledge of weather, believers in God should not be surprised that physical elements respond to their Creator.

Next, David summarizes his deliverance from enemies:

¹⁷ "He **sent** from above, He **took** me,
He **drew** me out of many waters.
¹⁸ He **delivered** me from my strong enemy,
From those who hated me;
For they were too strong for me.
¹⁹ They confronted me in the day of my calamity,
But the Lord was my **support.**
²⁰ He also **brought** me out into a broad place;
He **delivered** me because He delighted in me.

After the excitement of the previous scene, this passage paints an exquisite picture of gentle deliverance. God had thundered and shot arrows of lightning; now the Most High humbly reaches down from heaven and draws David "out of many waters."

God's wrath is for enemies and the unrighteous; His tender care is for His faithful ones. Notice the power of the parallel verbs: "sent," "took," "drew," and "delivered." The Hebrew verb for "drew" occurs only three times in the Old Testament: here in verse 17, Psalm 18:16, and Exodus 2:10, when Pharaoh's daughter named her adopted son "Moses," because she drew him from the water.[21]

21   Youngblood 1071.

The water that should have killed Moses became his lifeline; generations later, God draws David from "many waters" or circumstances threatening death. In two lines of poetry, David connects his life with the life of God's faithful servant, Moses. God delivers David *from* death and *to* the kingship of Israel.

David is also rescued *from* his "strong enemy" and those who "hated" him—enemies too strong for him, but not for the LORD. God doesn't stop with a just a rescue from danger, however; he also delivers David *to* "a broad place," spacious and free of traps and snares.

David concludes that God "delighted" in him, showing mercy and favor. A comment about this same line in Psalm 18:19 seems appropriate before we move to the next section: "Those who trust in God are people who bring God great pleasure and joy. He loves them and acts in their behalf."[22]

Just Thinking . . .

1. Discuss the difference in tone between verses 8-16 and verses 17-20.

2. Why did God "delight" in David?

---

22   Cloer 229.

Chapter 5

The Song of David

Parts 2 and 3, Conclusion

The Song of David, Part 2

(2 Samuel 22:21-30)

In Part 2, David claims two related reasons for God's consistent deliverance on his part—his righteousness and his efforts to obey God's commands.[23]

> ²¹ The LORD **rewarded** me according to my **righteousness;**
> According to the **cleanness of my hands**
> He has **recompensed** me.
> ²² For **I have kept the ways of the LORD,**
> And **have not wickedly departed from my God.**
> ²³ For all His judgments *were* before me;
> And *as for* His statutes, I did not depart from them.
> ²⁴ **I was also blameless** before Him,
> And **I kept myself from my iniquity.**
> ²⁵ Therefore the LORD has **recompensed me according to my righteousness,**
> According to my **cleanness in His eyes.**

Three times in this short passage, David says that God "rewarded" or "recompensed" him for his righteousness. Is David claiming perfection? Have his good works and careful attention to God's Law earned deliverance? Not at all. Instead, he knows God is always on the side of righteousness, and David has always tried to obey God.

We know that Abraham "believed in the LORD, and He accounted it to him for righteousness" (Genesis 15:6). In a similar way, "There is therefore now no condemnation to those who are in Christ Jesus, who do not walk according to the flesh, but according to the Spirit" (Romans 8:1). Having "put on Christ" in baptism (Galatians 3:27), Christians "wear" His righteousness by "putting on" His qualities (Colossians 3:12-14).

Reward for righteousness is a biblical principle that David understood well. When he had an opportunity to kill King Saul, he chose not to do so. Notice his reasoning:

> ²³ May the LORD repay every man *for* his righteousness and his faithfulness;
> for the LORD delivered you into *my* hand today, but I would not stretch out my
> hand against the LORD's anointed. And indeed, as your life was valued much
> this day in my eyes, so let my life be valued much in the eyes of the LORD, and
> let Him deliver me out of all tribulation (1 Samuel 26:23-24).

---

23   Youngblood 1071.

God knew David's heart, and by God's own witness, He understood David's meaning when he claimed to be righteous, clean, and blameless.[24] In the total context of his life, David became the standard by which all other kings of Israel were judged. Solomon's heart "was not loyal to the LORD his God, as *was* the heart of his father David" (1 Kings 11:4). Of Jeroboam, among other kings, God said, "You have not been as My servant David, who kept My commandments and who followed Me with all his heart, to do only *what was* right in My eyes" (1 Kings 14:7-8).

What about David's adultery and murder? If scholars are correct, David wrote this song before he committed these terrible sins. Later, God acknowledged David's righteousness "except in the matter of Uriah the Hittite" (1 Kings 15:5), and God forgave David when he repented (Psalm 51; 2 Samuel 12:9-14).

Just Thinking . . .

1. In verses 21-25, David states that he is righteous, clean, and blameless in God's eyes, and that he has kept God's statutes. Is he bragging? Does God generally reward people for being good?

2. How can we as Christians "live righteously" without being "self-righteous"?

In verses 26-30, David addresses God's mercy and justice.

> [26] With the **merciful** You will show Yourself merciful;
> With a **blameless** man You will show Yourself blameless;
> [27] With the **pure** You will show Yourself pure;
> And with the **devious** You will show Yourself **shrewd.**
> [28] You will **save the humble people;**
> But Your eyes *are* on the **haughty,** *that* You may **bring *them* down.**
>
> [29] For You *are* my **lamp,** O LORD;
> The LORD shall **enlighten** my darkness.
> [30] For by You I can **run** against a troop;
> By my God I can **leap** over a wall.

Having described God at length, David now speaks directly to God in second person, noting His positive response to the godly and His negative response to the ungodly. Faithful followers of God will reflect—or at least attempt to reflect—God's own character by being merciful, blameless (without fault), and pure. God recognizes their efforts and blesses them with the same qualities. David's words provide a hint of Jesus' teaching in the Beatitudes in Matthew 5:7-8.

However, devious people can expect a shrewd response from God: He will expose their foolish or evil behaviors. As a result, God will deliver humble people who realize how much they need Him and bring down haughty people who don't acknowledge Him. The Hebrew verbs in verse 28 are similar to those in Hannah's description of the LORD who "brings low and lifts up" in 1 Samuel 2:7.[25]

Just Thinking . . .

1. In a time and place when people worshiped many gods made of stone or wood, how does David present God as different from the pagan idols?

2. What do verses 26-28 tell us about how God interacts with people?

---

24   Youngblood 1072.
25   Youngblood 1073.

In verse 29, David continues to describe faithful servants reflecting traits of God by calling God "my lamp" who "shall enlighten my darkness." Psalm 18:28 states, "For You will light my lamp." Once, in 2 Samuel 21:15-17, King David was nearly killed during a battle with the Philistines. Alarmed by the close call, his men said David shouldn't fight in battles, "lest you quench the lamp of Israel." As the righteous leader of Israel, David was a good influence, but he acknowledged God as the source of any light or goodness in his life.[26] God "enlightens" David's "darkness;" He gives wisdom in a confused, ungodly world.

This section ends with an exuberant burst of invincibility. With God's help, David is sure he can do anything—run fearlessly toward the enemy (as he ran toward Goliath) or leap easily over obstacles. His close relationship with God empowers David in every righteous act.

Just Thinking . . .

1. David credits God as the lamp or light in his life in verse 29, but David's men call him the "lamp of Israel." In what ways should a godly leader exhibit "light" to those he leads? When did David fail in this responsibility?

2. Find at least three references that show Jesus' use of the imagery of light.

The Song of David, Part 3

(2 Samuel 22:31-46)

Part 3 consists of verses 31-46, explaining how God works out His deliverance. David repeats some descriptive words from verses 2-4.

> [31] *As for* God, His **way** *is* **perfect;**
> The **word** of the LORD *is* **proven;**
> He *is* a **shield** to all who trust in Him.

The word "God" as used in the first line is literally "the God," as in there is no other.[27] Since most ancient civilizations worshiped multiple gods, David's assertion of One True God restates the Bible's theme of the unique God revealing His character to His created beings. God's uniqueness includes His perfect way, His proven word, and His protective shield for those who trust Him. "Perfect" means "entire, unblemished, or complete," and "way" literally means "road" and figuratively means "a course of action."[28] If David walks in God's way, his way will also be perfect or complete.

"Word" can mean "commandment" or "speech;" God's word is pure or flawless, like precious metal that has been "proven" or "refined."[29] God protects His own, like a shield. Without God, David has nothing; with God, David needs nothing else.

David begins the next section with two questions:

> [32] For who *is* God, except the LORD?
> And who *is* a rock, except our God?

26   Cloer 231.
27   Youngblood 1074.
28   *Strong's Concordance with Hebrew and Greek Lexicon* online: "tamiym" # 8549 and "derek" # 1870.
www.eliyah.com/lexicon.html
29   Youngblood 1074.

³³ God *is* my **strength *and* power,**
And He **makes my way perfect.**

³⁴ He makes my feet like the *feet* of deer,
And sets me on my high places.
³⁵ He **teaches** my hands to make war,
So that my arms can bend a bow of bronze.

³⁶ You have also given me the **shield** of Your salvation;
Your **gentleness** has made me great.
³⁷ You enlarged my path under me;
So my feet did not slip.

"Who is God, except the LORD?" Of course, the answer is "No one." David's confidence flows from frequent experience with God's powerful deliverance. God blessed David with strength, agility, and skill in fighting. Bending "a bow of bronze" is hyperbole (poetic exaggeration) since bows were always made of wood, not metal.

In verse 33, the Hebrew word translated "perfect" can also be translated "blameless," which means "without legitimate accusation." Psalm 18:32 reads, "*It is* God who arms me with strength, And makes my way perfect." The KJV uses "girdeth me," suggesting God has wrapped David in strength like a garment."³⁰ As long as David walks in God's way, he will be victorious. Centuries later, the apostle John would write that followers of Jesus who "walk in the light as He is in the light" would experience His cleansing of sin—an even greater victory (1 John 1:7).

Verses 36 and 37 repeat the shield image and the idea of God gently reaching down to deliver David, ensuring victory and safe passage. His path is wide and free of anything that would cause him to stumble.

The "gentleness" of God that makes David "great" contrasts sharply with the language in verses 38-43. Notice the strong verbs describing David's victory:

³⁸ I have **pursued** my enemies and **destroyed** them;
Neither did I turn back again till they were **destroyed.**
³⁹ And I **have destroyed** them and **wounded** them,
So that they **could not rise;**
They have **fallen** under my feet.
⁴⁰ For You have **armed** me with strength for the battle;
You have **subdued** under me those who rose against me.
⁴¹ You have also **given me the necks** of my enemies,
So that I **destroyed** those who hated me.
⁴² They looked, but *there was* none to save;
Even to the LORD, but He did not answer them.
⁴³ Then I **beat** them as fine as the dust of the earth;
I **trod** them like dirt in the streets,
And I **spread** them out.

First David records his actions; he relentlessly and thoroughly destroys his enemies. Then in verses 40-41, he credits God with subduing his enemies. The phrase "given me the necks of my enemies" is similar to language used in Genesis 49:8 and Joshua 10:22-25, showing dominance of the victor.

---

30   Cloer 233.

Verse 42 suggests that when David's enemies realize they cannot win the battle, they seek God's help, but He doesn't answer. This line echoes verses 27 and 28; God protects His faithful ones but brings down those who have rejected Him.

David's destruction of the enemy is so complete that he literally returns them to dust. While we might be shocked that David would boast about killing and humiliating even an enemy, remember that in the Old Testament God often instructed His people to destroy the idol worshipers who threatened them (Deuteronomy 13:15; 20:16-18; Joshua 8:26; 9:24).

The following verses list the benefits of God's deliverance:

> [44] You have also **delivered** me from the strivings of my people;
> You have **kept me** as the head of the nations.
> A people I have not known shall **serve** me.
> [45] The foreigners **submit** to me;
> As soon as they hear, they **obey** me.
> [46] The foreigners **fade** away,
> And **come frightened** from their hideouts.

Other nations now serve David, but the first line of verse 44 is confusing. The corresponding verse in Psalm 18:43 reads, "the strivings of the people," but in this version, David uses "my people." Why would his own people strive with him?

Perhaps he refers to the conflict that arose after the death of King Saul. When David was anointed king over Judah in Hebron, Saul's general Abner made Ishbosheth king over Israel (2 Samuel 2:4-11). War between David and Saul's followers continued for several years (3:1; 5:1-5), but God continued to deliver David so he could rule all the tribes of Israel.

David describes allegiance from foreign nations in verses 45 and 46. As usual, the verbs drive the poetic imagery: foreigners "submit," "obey," "fade," and "come frightened." Resistance is futile against God's anointed king, as suggested by "As soon as they hear, they obey." David didn't always have to fight; some yielded to him based on knowledge of the power and success God had given him.[31]

God delivered all of David's enemies into his hand, making him one of the most powerful kings of all time, and David gave God the glory.

Just Thinking . . .

1. Discuss the language used in verses 38-43 to describe David's victories in battle. Why did God insist on total destruction of pagan cultures?

2. How does this description compare to modern wars?

---

31   Cloer 237.

Conclusion

(2 Samuel 22:47-51)

David concludes with more praise for God, speaking first about Him and then to Him:

> [47] **The LORD lives!**
> **Blessed** *be* my Rock!
> Let God be **exalted,**
> The Rock of my salvation!
> [48] *It is* God who **avenges** me,
> And **subdues** the peoples under me;
> [49] He **delivers** me from my enemies.
> You also **lift me up** above those who rise against me;
> You have **delivered** me from the violent man.

David's initial "how-dare-you" reaction to Goliath's challenge in 1 Samuel 17:26 formed the basis of his life-long confidence in God. As the king of Israel, David still knows without a doubt that "The LORD lives!" He therefore blesses, praises, and exalts "The Rock of my salvation!"

David didn't take vengeance on his enemies; God did. David didn't subdue the peoples; God did. God delivered him and lifted him up, saving him from all enemies.

The last two verses reinforce the reason for the song:

> [50] **Therefore I will give thanks to You, O LORD,**
> among the Gentiles, And **sing praises** to Your name.
>
> [51] *"He is* the **tower of salvation** to His king, And **shows**
> **mercy** to His anointed, To David and his descendants
> forevermore."

The word "therefore" means, "as a result of, for this reason, or consequently." The verbal equivalent of a door hinge, "therefore" swings the reader's mind back to all that has been said up to this point and then swings forward to the final climax, as if to say, "Now you know why!"

And so we do. For David, giving thanks and singing praises to the LORD who delivered, rescued, and saved him repeatedly just comes naturally. He can never repay God's marvelous acts, but he can express gratitude and praise to God with a beautiful song.

David doesn't limit his offering of praise to the nation of Israel; he wants everyone to praise God, even "among the Gentiles." The apostle Paul quotes Psalm 18:49 in Romans 15:9 as proof that God offers salvation to everyone.

Verse 51 may apply to David and to Christ. God promised in His covenant with David to establish his throne forever (2 Samuel 7:16). David is the anointed king of Israel; Christ is the eternal Anointed One. Indeed, in his Pentecost sermon Peter quoted freely from Psalm 16, recognizing David's prophecy of the coming of the resurrected Christ (Acts 2:22-32). Peter also referred to Christ as the promised fulfillment of the oath sworn to David regarding his descendants.

Application: A Portrait of God

One lifelong goal for every Christian is to know God better each day. Too often, we settle for knowledge about God—facts and commandments—without taking time to discover the beautiful nuances of God's character.

David knew God. In his song of deliverance, David painted a personal word-portrait of God. David's natural talent with words bloomed in his lifetime interaction with God and matured under the Holy Spirit's inspiration to preserve these praises and descriptions for all generations.

What characteristics of God does David reveal? We see God as powerful but not cruel; He uses His power for His good will and justice. He knows everything, but He forgives His repentant children. He is stronger than anyone or anything else in the heavens or on the earth, yet He is humble and gentle, stooping down to the earth to help us. He is kind and wise, understanding that dramatic action on a battlefield will get our attention, but we will be better served and saved by the Savior, "For He made Him who knew no sin to be sin for us, that we might become the righteousness of God in Him" so we could spend eternity with Him (2 Corinthians 5:21).

God delivered David *from* his enemies and delivered him *to* the kingship of Israel. He delivered David *from* the pride of self-confidence that so often causes humans to stumble; He delivered him *to* the certainty of God-confidence in righteous living.

In our own battles against sin, we learn from David that no giant is bigger than God; no army is stronger. Our archenemy Satan would have us believe that we can't win; David's life is testimony to the contrary—in fact, Christ has already won the battle for us.

No wonder David ends his song by emphasizing that God is "the **tower of salvation . . .** [Who] **shows mercy** to His anointed, To David and his descendants forevermore." And we as Christians are the most blessed of all, as David's spiritual descendants, wearing the name of the Eternal King, Jesus the Christ.

Just Thinking . . .

1. Most of us will probably never fight on a battlefield or become rulers of a nation. Why do we as Christians need to understand David's song of deliverance?

2. How can knowing God and Christ help us fight our daily battles aagainst Satan?

Chapter 6
David's Song of Suffering and Salvation:
Psalm 22, Part 1

God's Covenant with David

Nathan the prophet walked with King David through his new house. After years of living in mountain caves and desert camps, David now had a home big enough for his family and grand enough for, well, a king. In fact, as king of Israel and Judah, David had everything—peace and security in Jerusalem, loyal soldiers to lead into battle if enemies should threaten, respect from his people, and ample tribute from the nations he had conquered. God had blessed him beyond all expectations, but there was one more thing David wanted. He had thought about it for a long time; now he decided to mention it to Nathan.

"It's not right; I dwell in a house of cedar, but the ark of God dwells in a tent."

Nathan understood the gratitude and faith within David's heart; why shouldn't he build a house for God? "The LORD is with you; do all that is in your heart." But that night, God spoke to Nathan with a message for His servant David:

"You wish to build a house for Me? I have never dwelt in a house nor wanted one; I have moved about in a tent with My people Israel and never asked them to build Me a house. And have I not brought you from the sheepfold to rule Israel? I have been with you; I have cut off all your enemies and made you a great name.

"Indeed, I will make a house for you. When you rest with your fathers, I will set up your seed, from your body, and I will establish his kingdom. He shall build a house for My name, and I will establish the throne of his kingdom forever. I will be his Father, and he shall be My son."

David listened to Nathan, first with disappointment and then with humility. The message continued with a warning. "If he commits iniquity, I will chasten him with the rod of men and with the blow of the sons of men. But my mercy shall not depart from him, as I took it from Saul. Your house and kingdom—your throne—shall be established forever."

For a long moment, David couldn't speak. He could see in his mind the great temple he wanted to build for the LORD: flawless stones, dazzling white in the sun; gold leaf and cedar; intricate carvings and tapestry work. His heart ached to build it—but God said no. Beyond the negative, however, David found consolation: "Your son . . . your seed . . . forever."

He thought of his dear friend Jonathan, Saul's son, who would have been king had Saul obeyed God. Chosen to succeed Saul, David now had the assurance that one of his sons would succeed him, and more than that, his heirs would continue to rule Israel for generations; his throne would be established forever!

Overwhelmed with the implications, David began to pray: "Who am I, O Lord GOD? And what is my house that You have brought me this far? For there is none like You, nor is there any God besides You . . . And who is like Your people, like Israel, the one nation on the earth whom God went to redeem for Himself as a people, to make for Himself a name—and to do for Yourself great and awesome deeds for Your land—before Your people whom You redeemed for Yourself from Egypt, the nations, and their gods?"

He continued to pray, magnifying God's name. "And let the house of Your servant David be established before You . . . . let it please You to bless the house of Your servant . . . for You, O Lord GOD, have spoken it, and with Your blessing let the house of Your servant be blessed forever."

When he finished his prayer, David continued to think about the great gift God had given Him—a promise, a covenant that would ensure his legacy—and he marveled at God's ability to deny his heart's desire and then replace it with something greater—his descendent on a throne, forever! (Based on 2 Samuel 7).

God's Promise

Soon after the first sin in the Garden of Eden, God promised that His Anointed One, Messiah, would "bruise the head" of the serpent (Genesis 3:15). God consistently renewed His promise in covenants with Abraham, Isaac, Jacob, the children of Israel, and now, David. Typically, covenants had partial fulfillment during the chosen person's lifetime with complete fulfillment far in the future.

God tells David that he will have a son who will inherit his throne and build a house (temple) for God; but many years after David dies, God would build a house (kingdom) for David's descendant that would last forever. Though David probably didn't grasp the full meaning of an eternal throne or the cost of establishing it, we know this king is Messiah (Christ), the Eternal King and Savior, Lord Jesus.

Just Thinking . . .

1. An antitype is a person or thing represented or foreshadowed by an earlier type or symbol. How is Christ an antitype of David?

2. Consider David's roles as shepherd, king, and prophet; look for references to Christ in these roles (John 10:11-14; Luke 24:18-20; John 18:37).

A Telescope and a Testimony

Sometime—maybe months, maybe years—after he learned of his legacy from God, David wrote Psalm 22. Unlike the jubilant songs about rescue from tyrants or personal despair, this psalm breaks our hearts. First it brings us to tears of grief and then to tears of joy. It sings of God's greatest deliverance—rescue *from* the worst enemy, Satan, and his cruelest weapon, sin—and *to* redemption and eternal reward.

Psalm 22 also reveals David's role as a prophet—a person who "speaks forth" the message of God and sometimes foretells the future. He may not fully understand these glimpses of the future; Peter wrote that those "who prophesied of the grace that would come to you" wanted to know the when and how of salvation, even as they spoke "beforehand the sufferings of Christ and the glories that would follow" (1 Peter 1:10-12).

In Psalm 22, the first-person narration unfolds the scene at the cross with the graphic detail of an eye-witness account, as if David had peered through a telescope into the distant future and then recorded what he saw. It describes suffering so intense we can hardly bear to read the pain-drenched words; then it carries us to a triumph so sublime that the writer can scarcely describe it.

Some scholars believe the events transpiring in the psalm had to come from a specific, personal persecution that caused God to abandon David. Yet nothing recorded about David's life suggests persecution this intense; even when Saul pursued him relentlessly, David always had family and loyal friends to encourage him; he always trusted in God's deliverance. Concerning this conflict between prophecy and personal experience, Eddie Cloer writes,

> The best explanation of this interpretative difficulty seems to be the
> view that the psalm has its roots in David's own trial of fire, but its

language reaches beyond his experiences to the sufferings of Christ.

While David may have understood that he was writing in exaggerated, poetic language about a bitter experience, he was in fact—by the guidance of the Holy Spirit—portraying the actual sufferings of Jesus in pictorial prophecy.[32]

David, being human, probably had experiences that caused him to feel abandoned or to worry that God might leave him. However, Psalm 22 also contains David's testimony of steadfast belief in God's faithfulness. Part 1 is a lament, a description of the believer's fear of the worst possible situation—life without God. Part 2 is a song of thanksgiving for the believer's greatest joy—life with God through redemption.

Part 1: The Lament

(Verses 1-21)

Verses 1 and 2 begin the lament with the familiar words of Christ's anguished cry from the cross, recorded in Matthew 27:46 and Mark 15:34:

> My God, My God, why have You **forsaken Me?**
> Why are You **so far from helping Me,**
> And **from the words of My groaning?**
> [2] O My God, I **cry** in the **daytime**, but You do not hear;
> And in the **night** season, and **am not silent.**

David, however, intensifies the cry through repetition. Three times he appeals to "My God," emphasizing the Father/Son relationship. Three times he questions God's abandonment. Faced with the absence of God, David expresses disbelief, as if saying, "God has always heard me; why doesn't He hear me now?" Though God is silent, the cries continue day and night.

What David sees in prophecy, we see as history. "The words of My groaning" should call to mind the Savior's impassioned prayers in Gethsemane when He was in extreme agony and distress, "exceedingly sorrowful, even to death" (Matthew 26:36-46; Luke 22:39-45). On the cross, Jesus expressed despair when He called out, "My God, My God, why have You forsaken Me?" God turned away when Christ bore in His flesh all the sins of all who had ever lived and all who ever will live, including my sins and yours (2 Corinthians 5:21).

Despite the agony of abandonment, David praises God and reminds Him of rescues in the past:

> [3] But You *are* **holy,**
> **Enthroned in the praises of Israel.**
> [4] Our fathers **trusted** in You;
> They **trusted**, and You delivered them.
> [5] They cried to You, and were delivered;
> They **trusted** in You, and were not ashamed.

Verse 3 describes God as "holy" and therefore worthy of praise. The praises of Israel are "like a huge cloud . . . received by God, who allows it to surround His throne as acceptable worship . . . . It is as if His throne is lifted up by that cloud."[33] Three times David records that Israel's trust in God was rewarded with deliverance; God is faithful, he reasons, so God will deliver again.

As the psalm continues, we begin to understand the emptiness and horror of life without God.

---

32   Cloer 282.
33   Cloer 283.

6 But I *am* a worm, and no man;
A reproach of men, and despised by the people.
7 All those who see Me ridicule Me;
They shoot out the lip, they shake the head, *saying,*
8 'He trusted in the LORD, let Him rescue Him;
Let Him deliver Him, since He delights in Him!'

Without God, the sufferer feels less than human, "a worm;" one of the lowliest of God's creatures, it is something often crushed and forgotten. No one shows respect or offers help; instead, all ridicule and despise him.

The Sunday before His death, Jesus rode into Jerusalem on a donkey as multitudes called Him "Son of David," a description of the Messiah (Matthew 21:1-9). Another crowd stood before Pilate a few days later and demanded the release of Barabbas, a murderer, and the crucifixion of Jesus, demonstrating how much Jesus was "despised" (27:15-22; Mark 15:6-15). Imagine preferring a convicted murderer over Jesus after he had healed, comforted, and taught them about God's kingdom!

Just Thinking . . .

1. Review verse 6 of David's lament. What kind of distress would cause a man to feel like a worm?

2. Though sinless, Jesus was despised and treated as a vile criminal. Today, men and women are still made in God's image, yet they often ignore that quality and live immoral lives. What do they need in order to change and become God's children?

Verse 8 mocks faith in God. The first line can be literally translated as "Roll [thy care] upon the LORD: let Him deliver him."[34] Matthew 27:39 speaks of those "who passed by [the cross]" blaspheming Jesus, and verses 41-43 tell us that the chief priests, scribes, and elders reviled Him with words similar to Psalm 22:8. Ironically, the religious leaders who were responsible for killing Jesus also confirmed Him as Messiah by using David's words of prophecy.

In the next passage, David pleads for help based on his lifelong faith in God:

9 But You *are* He who took Me out of the womb;
You made Me trust while on My mother's breasts.
10 I was cast upon You **from birth.**
From My mother's womb
You have been My God.
11 **Be not far from Me,**
For trouble is near;
For there is none to help.

David credits God with creating him and instilling trust within in him even as an infant. This may seem like exaggeration for poetic effect; perhaps David believed God had protected him from his earliest days, so why would He desert him now?[35]

---

34   G. Rawlinson, *Psalms*, The Pulpit Commentary, ed. H.D.M. Spence and Joseph S. Exell, vol.8 (Grand Rapids, Mich.: Wm. B. Eerdmans Publishing Co., 1950) 152.
35   Cloer 285.

In modern terms, think of a little child reared in a godly home and taught from infancy about God—learning early to pray and sing songs like "Jesus Loves Me," always going to Sunday school but also learning Scripture at home, surrounded by good examples of Christian family and friends. If that child continued to grow and live in faith all her life, she could say truthfully, "I have known God ever since I was born; I don't remember not knowing God."

Apply the description to Jesus. Because He was chosen to redeem the world from sin before creation, God loved Him even then (1 Peter 1:20; John 17:24). He was conceived in the womb of a virgin and dedicated to God from birth (Luke 1:35; 2:21-22, 40). He understood from childhood that He must serve His Father (vv. 49, 52). Throughout His ministry, Jesus often sought comfort and wisdom in solitary prayer (Mark 1:35; Luke 9:18). We could say, "From the first dawn of consciousness God was His God."[36]

The plaintive tone of verse 11 rends the heart as we remember that His disciples desert Him when the soldiers arrest Him (Matthew 26:55-56). Ultimately, the most reliable Helper also turns away (27:46, 50).

Until He went to the cross burdened with sins not His own, Jesus had never known the absence of God. Because He died on the cross, Jesus knows exactly how all people on earth will feel—lost, abandoned, hopeless—if they remain in their sins.

Now David presents several vivid images to describe the terror and despair of being surrounded by enemies:

> [12] Many **bulls** have surrounded Me;
> Strong bulls of Bashan have encircled Me.
> [13] They gape at Me with their mouths,
> **Like a raging and roaring lion.**

Bashon was an area of rich pastureland east of the Sea of Galilee noted for producing good cattle and exceptionally strong, vicious bulls. They could easily gore or trample a man; they are as dangerous as roaring lions.

> [14] I am **poured out** like water,
> And all My **bones are out of joint**;
> My **heart is like wax**;
> It has melted within Me.
> [15] My **strength is dried** up like a potsherd,
> And My **tongue clings to My jaws**;
> You have brought Me to the **dust of death.**

Verses 14 and 15 describe the effects of physical torture on the human body. "Poured out like water" suggests extreme weakness and wasted strength. Imagine Jesus after His arrest:

- He has nothing to eat or drink after Thursday night.

- He is exhausted from prayer in Gethsemane.

- He is dragged through the streets to the Jewish leaders, to Pilate, to Herod, and back to Pilate.

- He is taunted and tortured by soldiers.

---

36   Rawlinson 152.

- He is brutally flogged and forced to carry His cross to Golgotha.

- He is weak and wasted physically, as formless as melted wax, with no "heart" to live.

Then they nail Him to the cross where He suffers for six hours, with His bones "out of joint" from the strain of body weight suspended from nails and dehydration creating more weakness and excruciating thirst. A potsherd is a piece of broken clay pottery, dry and useless. No wonder Jesus said, "I thirst" (John 19:28). Worst of all, God has allowed this to happen: "You have brought me to the dust of death."

The lament continues for five more verses, but let us pause here and think about the last line of verse 15. Often today, atheists and others without faith justify their unbelief with the criticism that "a loving God would not allow suffering." Yet it is clear throughout the Bible that God not only allows suffering as a consequence of free will but also uses it to refine and purify His children.

Indeed, God required suffering and sacrifice from His own Son as payment for the sins of mankind. Hebrews 5:8 reminds us that Jesus learned obedience through suffering. In the Garden of Gethsemane, Jesus asked God, "Let this cup pass from me . . . nevertheless, not as I will, but as You will" (Matthew 26:39). Jesus understood what was at stake, and He was willing to endure suffering once so that all people could have access to salvation.

Just Thinking . . .

1. Verses 1-15 have obvious references to the suffering of Christ. Is David also describing his own suffering?

2. If so, what events in David's life might have caused him to feel abandoned by God?

Chapter 7
David's Song of Suffering and Salvation:
Psalm 22

Part 1 Continued and Part 2

Part 1: The Lament: Verses 16-18

Verses 16-18 present more images of enemies and pain:

> ¹⁶ For **dogs** have surrounded Me;
> The congregation of the wicked has enclosed Me.
> **They pierced My hands and My feet;**
> ¹⁷ I can count all My bones.
> They look *and* stare at Me.
> ¹⁸ They **divide My garments among them,**
> And for My clothing they cast lots.

In ancient times, dogs were seldom kept as pets. They were unclean animals that ran in packs, surviving on garbage and carrion. To be called a dog was an insult; to be surrounded by wild dogs meant a horrible death. "Congregation of the wicked" suggests a group of wicked, bloodthirsty men who might act like wild dogs.[37] The Jewish leaders demeaned Jesus by turning over the sinless Son of God to powerful, crude pagans for execution.

The third line of verse 16, "They pierced My hands and My feet," is interesting because in the original Hebrew, the phrase has no verb. It literally reads, "Like lions, my hands and my feet," comparing wounds of the hands and feet with bites made by the sharp teeth of lions. Early translators supplied the word "pierced" because it fit with the noun "lions" as a method of torture, and some English translations include the word "lions."[38]

The Roman style of crucifixion was unknown in David's time. Jewish law executed blasphemers by stoning and then impaling the corpse "on a tree" or pole as further humiliation (Deuteronomy 21:22-23). Yet David prophesied about Christ's pierced hands and feet. Also, brutal treatment accents or exposes His bones, producing a skeletal appearance. Bystanders stare and gawk at him, despising Him as a criminal

Verse 18 records the dividing of the condemned man's clothing among His executioners, verified by all four gospel writers (Matthew 27:35; Mark 15:24; Luke 23:34; and John 19:23-24).

Just Thinking . . .

1. David compares the enemies to dogs, bulls, and lions. How are the men who crucified Jesus like these animals?

2. Why did the soldiers divide Jesus' clothing?

---

37   Cloer 286.
38   Cloer 287.

Despite physical and mental agony, David continues to pray for deliverance.

> [19] But You, O LORD, **do not be far from Me;**
> O My Strength, **hasten** to help Me!
> [20] **Deliver Me** from the sword,
> My **precious** *life* **from the power of the dog.**
> [21] **Save Me** from the lion's mouth
> And from the horns of the wild oxen!
>
> You have answered Me.

Death is near; He has no strength except in God. David repeats the three images of enemies in reverse order: dog, lion, and wild oxen (similar to bulls). "Sword" and "power of the dog" could refer to the authority of the Roman soldiers.

The New American Standard Bible translates verses 20 and 21 as "Deliver **my soul** from the sword, **My only** *life* from the power of the dog. Save me from the lion's mouth; From the horns of the wild oxen You answer me." Both "precious" and "only life" suggest the uniqueness of an "only" child of God.[39]

Since "soul" and "life" are sometimes used interchangeably in Scripture, could there be a subtle shift in emphasis here? Instead of seeking deliverance *from* death, does David realize that in the case of Messiah, the Man on the cross must be delivered *to* death? Is that why He now says, "You have answered Me"?

Though enemies still surround Jesus, though Satan believes he has triumphed over Him, God has not forsaken Him permanently. Rawlinson suggests that

> The conviction suddenly comes to the Sufferer that he is heard. . . .
> The despondent mood has passed away. He is not forsaken. He has
> One to help. In one way or another he knows himself—feels himself—
> delivered; and he passes from despair and agony into a condition of
> perfect peace, and even exultation. He passes, in fact, from death to life,
> from humiliation to glory; and at once he proceeds to show forth his
> thankfulness by a burst of praise.[40]

Jesus once told His disciples,

> [24]If anyone desires to come after Me, let him deny himself, and take up
> his cross, and follow Me. [25]For whoever desires to save his life will lose
> it, but whoever loses his life for My sake will find it. [26]For what profit is
> it to a man if he gains the whole world, and loses his own soul? Or what
> will a man give in exchange for his soul? (Matthew 16:24-26).

In reference to Psalm 22, we might ask, "Who would be willing to give his physical life for the souls of the whole world?" Only Messiah. Only the Son of God. By dying, He has completed the work God sent Him to do.

---

39   Cloer 288.
40   Rawlinson 154.

Just Thinking . . .

1. Verse 21 signals a change in attitude as the psalm moves from lament to praise. In what sense did God "answer" or deliver Christ even though He allowed Him to die?

2. In what sense do we "die" when we become Christians?

Part 2: The Song of Thanksgiving for Deliverance

(Verses 22-31)

The change in mood from verse 21 to verse 22 is so abrupt that some believe David wrote two separate songs and then combined them later. Part one is obviously God-inspired prophecy, and David probably didn't completely understand all the implications of what he was guided to write. Part 2, however, demonstrates that David did understand at least one aspect of the prophecy—that his descendant, Messiah, was delivered *to* death so that all people could have the opportunity for deliverance *from* sin and *to* eternal life.

Part 2 presents the joyful part of the same story, contrasting the sacrificial suffering with the blessed reward. It begins with a declaration and call to praise God.

> 22 I will **declare Your name** to My brethren;
> In the midst of the assembly I will **praise You.**
> 23 You who fear the LORD, praise Him!
> All you descendants of Jacob, **glorify Him,**
> And fear Him, all you offspring of Israel!

The word translated "declare" can also be translated as "score with a mark as a tally or record, to inscribe, recount, to celebrate or commune."[41] David (and by extension of prophecy, Christ) is going "on the record" with the Name (authority) of God in the assembly or congregation of brethren. In contrast with the individual plea for help in verses 1 and 2, David now calls all of Jacob's faithful descendants to glorify God. Why?

> 24 For He has not despised nor abhorred the affliction
> of the afflicted;
> Nor has He hidden His face from Him;
> But when **He cried to Him, He heard.**

God never fails to *hear* the cries for deliverance, but *deliverance comes in His time and for His purpose.* He turned away from the sin-laden Savior so His suffering could fulfill the work of redemption. Only when Christ had "poured out his soul unto death" could the Father exalt the Son through resurrection and then reunion in heaven (Isaiah 53:12; Philippians 2:8-11).

> 25 My **praise *shall be* of You** in the great assembly;
> I will pay My vows before those who fear Him.
> 26 The poor shall eat and be satisfied;
> Those who **seek Him will praise the LORD.**
> Let your heart live forever!

---

41   *Strong's Concordance with Hebrew and Greek Lexicon* online: "caphar" #5608. www.eliyah.com/lexicon. html

Even when God does not answer prayers immediately or as the petitioners had hoped, they should praise Him and fulfill their vows. David offers thanks for the great sacrifice witnessed only in prophecy, but he is confident God will fulfill His promised deliverance.

Just Thinking . . .

1. Discuss this comment about Psalm 22:25-26: "When one is in the valley of despair and his prayer is not heard, the next step is to praise God. Any time—even in the midst of an indescribable ordeal—is an appropriate time to give glory and thanks to God."[42]

2. What blessings might arise from praising God in the midst of suffering?

David also reveals that in the celebration to come, all nations will worship God—a contrast with Israel's worship in verses 3-5.

> [27] **All** the ends of the world
> **Shall remember and turn to the LORD,**
> And **all** the families of the nations
> **Shall worship before You.**
> [28] For the kingdom *is* the LORD's,
> And He rules over the nations.
>
> [29] **All the prosperous** of the earth
> Shall eat and worship;
> **All those who go down to the dust**
> **Shall bow before Him,**
> Even he who cannot keep himself alive.

The word translated "remember" carries the meaning of "recognize" or "call to remembrance." Through the chosen race of Israel, God sent Christ into the world, but all people are made in His image and have "eternity in their hearts" (Ecclesiastes 3:11). Messiah allows all to be drawn to Him, and even those who don't acknowledge God now will someday recognize and worship Him. Those who are prosperous will "eat and worship;" those near death will receive new hope.[43]

One last prophecy closes the psalm joyfully:

> [30] A **posterity** shall serve Him.
> It will be recounted of the Lord to **the next generation,**
> [31] **They will come and declare His righteousness** to a
> people who will be born,
> That **He has done this.**

Since God promised that David's seed would someday be enthroned forever, David probably envisioned an earthly kingdom. Certainly the first-century Jews expected Messiah to free them from Roman rule. Even the apostles missed the concept of a spiritual kingdom, asking Jesus, "Lord, will You at this time restore the kingdom to Israel?" before His ascension (Acts 1:6).

---

42 Cloer 293.
43 Cloer 291.

But David had at least a glimpse of God's greatest deliverance. Posterity means "seed;" future generations of David's descendants would serve the Lord. Each generation would tell the next of Christ's suffering and His death.

This teaching would go beyond David's family, beyond the Israelites. The word "declare" in verse 31 is from a different Hebrew word than the word translated "declare" in verse 22. This one means "to stand boldly out opposite, to manifest, to announce by word of mouth to one present, to certify."[44]

The apostles preached Jesus "boldly," though they were ordered to stop (Acts 4:18-20). They felt compelled to "manifest" the righteousness of Christ to everyone who would listen. Then the people they taught also taught others, year after year, generation after generation, "to a people who will be born" (Psalm 22:31; cf. 2 Timothy 2:2).

What did they teach, as one century passed into the next? "That He has done this." Christ completed the work of redemption. His suffering had a purpose: to bring all who are willing to repent and obey into a saved relationship with God. The last line of Psalm 22 corresponds to Christ's dying words on the cross: "It is finished."

So much time has passed since David sang his songs of deliverance and since the establishment of the church in the first century. Faith has ebbed and flowed, blossoming under persecution and faltering during prosperity. Think of the apostasy, the division, the Crusades, the Dark Ages, the Inquisition, the Reformation, and the Restoration as mankind alternately polluted and attempted to purify the kingdom of God on earth.

Through all these events, the simple gospel, the good news that God has a plan for man's salvation, has remained intact, inerrant, and embedded in the Bible, clear as day for seekers. So it has come down through the ages to us.

We are part of David's spiritual posterity; we know the fulfillment of prophecy. We have received salvation bought with innocent blood. With exuberant joy, we also can say, "He has done this!" His sacrifice redeemed us; His resurrection conquered death and assured eternal life for us.

Application: Sharing the Joy

There is another aspect of the joy predicted in Psalm 22. Hebrews 12:1-2 encourages Christians to "run with endurance the race that is set before us, looking unto Jesus, the author and finisher of our faith, who for **the joy that was set before Him** endured the cross, despising the shame, and has sat down at the right hand of the throne of God."

What was the joy set before Jesus while He suffered on the cross? Was it not the knowledge that millions upon millions of people would have the opportunity to become God's children? Jesus knew that once He finished His sacrifice, the gates of heaven would receive Him again, but He also knew that heaven would be the eternal home for many, many more.

As we imitate Jesus in submission to God, in suffering, and in attitude and action, should we not also imitate "the joy that was set before Him"? Should we not delight in sharing the gospel of Christ with everyone we meet?

---

44   *Strong's Concordance with Hebrew and Greek Lexicon* online: "nagad" #5046. www.eliyah.com/lexicon. html

Isaiah 55:3-4 speaks of David as "a witness to the people." Verses 11-12 read,

> [11] So shall My word be that goes forth from My mouth;
> It shall not return to Me void,
> But it shall accomplish what I please,
> And it shall prosper in the thing for which I sent it.
>
> [12] For you shall go out with joy,
> And be led out with peace;
> The mountains and the hills
> Shall break forth into singing before you,
> And all the trees of the field shall clap their hands.

Knowing His death would redeem mankind brought joy to Jesus and helped Him endure the suffering on the cross. That joy reached its peak on resurrection morning. The women who had followed Jesus even to the cross now came early to the tomb to anoint His dead body, but angels asked, "Why do you seek the living among the dead? He is not here, but is risen! (Luke 24:1-6,10; cf. Matthew 28:5-8). Surely Mary Magdalene's grief turned to joy when she wept in the garden and then saw Jesus alive! (John 20:11-18).

The gospel message should inspire joy in us as well. Like the women who ran from the tomb to tell the good news, we run today, eager to share, to teach, to live, to sacrifice, and to celebrate as our lives become songs of deliverance. We are saved, and we want others to be saved, for there is no greater joy than eternal life with God.

Just Thinking . . .

1. Read Hebrews 11:32-12:3. What is the joy set before Christ that helped Him endure the cross?

2. How are Christians today a part of the "posterity" that David talks about in Psalm 22:30? How do we participate in and react to the joy of salvation?

Chapter 8
The Song of Jonah
Jonah 2:1-9

The Not-so-Great Escape

Jonah stood on a pier in Joppa, weighing his options. He called to a man on the deck of the nearest ship. "Where are you bound?"

"Tarshish," he replied. "Where are you bound?"

Jonah boarded the ship, money in hand. "Tarshish will do. How much?"

The captain asked, "You don't care where you go? Where are you from?"

"Gath Hepher and Samaria."

The captain named a sum; Jonah paid it. Below deck, he found a makeshift bed. He settled in, thinking of God's words: "Go to Nineveh, that great city, and cry out against it; for their wickedness has come up before Me."

Jonah couldn't believe it—Nineveh? The Assyrian capital? They were pagans—worse— barbarians, cruel and wicked.[45] Why would God send him to heathens? As a prophet, Jonah had brought God's message to Jeroboam, king of Israel; despite his evil ways, God had allowed him to restore Israel's territory from Hamath to the Sea of the Arabah (2 Kings 14:23-25). Didn't that prove that the worst Israelite was better than the best man in Nineveh?

Among his angry thoughts, Jonah found guilt. Though Israel persisted in idol worship, God had shown mercy and protected Jonah. So why was he headed for Tarshish instead of Nineveh? He ignored the question and went to sleep.

The ship set sail; Jonah slept soundly for hours. He didn't hear the rising wind or the crashing waves or the frightened cries of the sailors. Then the captain shook him and shouted, "Wake up! Call on your god; maybe he will consider us so that we will not perish!"

---

45   Albert Ten Eyck Olmstead, *History of Assyria*, (New York: Charles Scribner's Sons, 1923) 645. Description of Assyria: "Ashur was its god, plunder its morality, material pleasure its ideal, cruelty and terror its means. No people was ever more abject than those of Ashur; no sovereigns were ever more despotic, more covetous, more vindictive, more pitiless, more proud of their crimes. Assyria sums up within herself all vices. Aside from bravery, she offers not a single virtue.

Jonah groped his way through darkness to the deck where the sailors surrounded him. "We have prayed to our gods, but they do not hear us. We must cast lots to find out who has angered them!" The lot fell on Jonah, as he knew it would. The sailors shouted their questions: "What is your occupation? Where is your country?"

"I am a Hebrew; and I fear the Lord, the God of heaven, who made the sea and the dry land."

His words terrified them. The sailors believed many gods ruled the elements—heaven, earth, sea, wind—but they had heard that the Hebrew God claimed to be the Creator and Controller of all elements. Could it be true? And if it were true, how could they ever appease a god so powerful?

Jonah knew. "This is my fault. Throw me into the sea; then it will be calm." The sailors protested. They rowed harder because they didn't want to invite further punishment for murder. But the tempest was too strong, so they threw Jonah overboard.

Immediately, the raging storm ceased. Stunned but relieved, they felt a great respect for the Lord, showing it with sacrifices and vows. And if any of them thought to look for the man who forfeited his life for them, it wouldn't have mattered. Jonah had disappeared. (Based Jonah 1).

Just Thinking . . .

1. Jonah boarded the ship to Tarshish to go "from the presence of the Lord" (1:3). As a prophet, he had to know he couldn't successfully run away from God (Psalm 139:7-12). Why do you think he tried?

2. How do people try to run from God today?

Jonah's Deliverance

We might doubt Jonah's good sense and even his faith when he ran from God, but we admire his repentance and courage. He knew God caused the storm to get his attention, and he couldn't let the sailors die because of his sin. He expected to die; perhaps he thought he deserved to die.

God, however, intended to deliver Jonah in a most unusual way. He didn't provide another ship to rescue him or give him the strength to swim to shore. Instead, God "prepared a great fish to swallow Jonah. And Jonah was in the belly of the fish three days and three nights" (v. 17).

Did God instantly create a special fish, or did He just make sure that a fish large enough to swallow a man was available? He was and is capable of either, but most commentaries favor the second view. As we have seen, God often uses natural elements for His purpose.

As Jonah sinks, drowning seems inevitable; then the fish swallows him, preserving his life. So, from the belly of a fish, Jonah prays (2:1).

Just Thinking . . .

1. When Jonah went into the sea, did he expect God to deliver him? How can you tell? At what point in the experience does Jonah begin to pray? How does prayer help him?

2. Compare the imagery in 2 Samuel 22:5-7 and Jonah 2:2-5.

Jonah's Prayer and Song

Jonah's prayer takes shape as a song that seeks and celebrates deliverance. When he hit the water, he had no hope of surviving, but in the strange, dark environment of the fish's belly, Jonah realizes God has delivered him, and he is grateful.

> [2]And he said, "I **cried out** to the Lord because of my affliction,
> And **He answered** me.
> Out of the belly of Sheol **I cried,**
> And **You heard** my voice.

Despite his disobedience, Jonah cries out to the Lord. Who else could save him? No one. Jonah doesn't describe the sensation of being swallowed by the fish; he was probably unconscious when it happened. How confused and frightened Jonah must have been when he woke up—relieved to be out of the sea's "wet darkness" but unsure of the "greater dry darkness" that now surrounds him like a "mysterious safety."[46] Recalling the terror of drowning, he assumes he is now in Sheol—the abode of the dead—but he is still alive!

Jonah seems surprised that God heard his cry. The Hebrew word translated "heard" means more than just noticing sound. Especially when coupled with God, it carries the idea of hearing intelligently or attentively.[47] "He [God] hears to answer, to rescue, to save. The Omnipresent did not lose sight of His servant even when he was beneath the waves of the ocean; and the All-gracious was not inattentive to his supplication . . . ."[48]

> [3]For **You cast me** into the deep,
> Into the heart of the seas,
> And the **floods surrounded** me;
> All Your billows and Your waves passed over me.

Jonah understands that God cast him into the water. He is not blaming so much as acknowledging God's control in this experience. Though he tried to run from God's presence, Jonah is surrounded by elements under God's control. Even at death's door, God is there.

> [4]Then I said, 'I have been **cast out** of Your sight;
> Yet I will look again toward Your holy temple.'

Jonah feels banished from God's sight. Before he realizes that isn't true, he decides to "look again toward Your holy temple," a reference to prayer. Faithful Israelites often prayed facing the temple in Jerusalem, even after it was destroyed, because it symbolized God's presence.

Jonah continues to describe the horrible experience of drowning.

> [5]The **waters surrounded** me, *even* to my soul;
> The **deep closed** around me;

---

46   H.L. Ellison, "Jonah" in *Daniel and the Minor Prophets,* The Expositor's Bible Commentary, ed. Frank E. Gaebelein, vol. 7 (Grand Rapids, Mich.: Zondervan,1985) 375.

47   *Strong's Concordance with Hebrew and Greek Lexicon* online: "shama" #8085. www.eliyah.com/lexicon.html

48   J.R. Thompson, "Jonah" in *Amos-Malachi,* The Pulpit Commentary, ed. H.D.M. Spence and Joseph S. Exell, vol.14 (Grand Rapids, Mich.: Wm. B. Eerdmans Publishing Co., 1950) 46.

Weeds were wrapped around my head.

> [6] I **went down** to the moorings of the mountains;
> The earth with its **bars** *closed* **behind me forever;**
> Yet **You have brought up my life** from the pit,
> O LORD, my God.

Jonah feels his life fading away. He sinks to the very bottom of the sea and feels seaweed around his head; he touches the "moorings" or roots of the mountains. He is beyond the hope of human help, and though "earth with its bars closed behind me forever" is figurative language, he might as well be locked out of life, for no one returns from the realm of the dead.[49]

Reading Jonah's song centuries later, we sense his panic; we weep for his hopeless, helpless situation. Then, just when he has given up, God delivers him from "the pit," a synonym for Sheol and for death.

> [7] When my **soul fainted** within me,
> **I remembered** the LORD;
> And my **prayer went** *up* to You,
> Into Your holy temple.

Half dead, Jonah remembers the LORD. Saved from drowning, he is still completely helpless. He can do nothing to save himself physically, but he hopes for spiritual deliverance. Quite literally, all he can do is pray, seeking the presence of God that he fled so thoughtlessly. At this low point, Jonah understands a principle he had tried to forget: ***He doesn't really want to be away from God.*** Jonah learns the hard way that the only thing worse than living without God is dying without God.

Perhaps remembering the pagan sailors desperately praying to their gods, Jonah includes a comment about idolatry in his song.

> [8] Those who regard worthless idols
> Forsake their own Mercy.

Jonah has also worshiped a worthless idol—the idol of self. Ironically, by choosing his own way and running from God, Jonah deserts the Source of mercy and goodness, just as the people of Israel had when they worshiped golden calves.

Now he knows better. He seeks atonement through sacrifice, but in his current situation, he has only a song to offer. He makes a vow to God and promises to pay it, assuming that God is going to complete his deliverance.

> [9] But I **will sacrifice** to You
> With the voice of thanksgiving;
> I **will pay** what I have vowed.
> Salvation *is* of the LORD."

---

49   Ellison, "Notes" 377-78.

Jonah doesn't explain his vow; perhaps he intends to obey God's original command or to offer an animal sacrifice. We don't need to know the details to understand that Jonah has learned the most important lesson from his experience: "Salvation is of the Lord." He gratefully acknowledges God as the only Source of salvation or deliverance—the only One worthy of praise. Jonah the rebellious prophet had knowledge about God; Jonah the delivered prophet has knowledge deepened by experience. Omnipresent God? He comes to the bottom of the sea. Omnipotent God? He conquers even death. Loving God? He loves Jonah enough to save him from spiritual death as well.

Just Thinking . . .

1. Jonah's song contains several images that occur in the Book of Psalms. What does the repetition of imagery in different biblical songs and poems tell us about the knowledge that different writers had of Old Testament Scripture? Consider these examples: Psalms 30:3; 42:7; 31:22; 5:7; and 69:1-2,30.

2. As Christians, we sometimes sin and then repent and seek God's forgiveness. How do we know that God will forgive us? Consider these verses: 1 John 1:5-9; 1 Timothy 1:15; and Matthew 6:14-15.

A Second Chance

After three days and nights, God speaks to the fish and it vomits Jonah out on the shore. We don't know how much time passes between his return to dry land and God's next communication with him, but this time when God says, "Go to Nineveh," Jonah goes!

We have only a brief account of the message God gave him: "Yet forty days and Nineveh shall be overthrown." As he walks through the city streets, people respond to his preaching by believing God; they fast and put on sackcloth to mourn their sins. The spontaneous response spreads quickly through this large city; even the king heeds Jonah's warning by leaving his throne and royal robe to wear coarse clothes and sit in ashes (3:6).

Then the king decrees that every man and beast must follow his example as they cry out to God and turn from evil and violent ways, for "Who can tell if God will turn and relent, and turn away from His fierce anger, so that we may not perish?" (v. 9).

And so He does: "Then God saw their works, that they turned from their evil way; and God relented from the disaster that He had said He would bring upon them, and He did not do it" (v. 10).

Jonah's Reaction

Having conducted the most successful mission trip on record, Jonah should have been thrilled. Instead, he is angry! His characterization of God borders on humor, like a left-handed compliment:

¹But it displeased Jonah exceedingly, and he became angry.

²So he prayed to the Lord, and said, "Ah, Lord, was not this what I said when I was still in my country? Therefore I fled previously to Tarshish; **for I know that You *are* a gracious and merciful God, slow to anger and abundant in lovingkindness, One who relents from doing harm.** ³Therefore

now, O Lord, please take my life from me, for *it is* better for
me to die than to live!" (4:2-3).

This from a man who recently thanked God for deliverance from death! He even criticizes God for being gracious and merciful!

Off he goes to sit on a hill above the city, pouting and hoping that God will destroy Nineveh after all. God provides a plant to shade him and then a worm to damage the plant. He sends a strong east wind; Jonah nearly faints from the sun's heat and wishes to die. God, however, expresses His pity for the people in the city (4:10-11).

The Book of Jonah ends without telling us if Jonah ever grasps the broader implications of these events in his life. We may see Jonah as a man of contradictions—a prophet who disobeys God, a man who is willing to give his life for pagan sailors caught in God's perfect storm, a man who accepts death but rejoices in deliverance. Though he succeeds in bringing an entire city of wicked people to their knees—literally—he resents God's compassion for those who repent.

We may shake our heads in disbelief, wondering how Jonah could be so hard-hearted and selfish. Yet even today, even among religious people, many have never learned the lesson that God taught to and through Jonah.

The Bigger Picture

God didn't pursue and rescue Jonah because no one else could go to Nineveh or because He wanted to punish His prophet. At the heart of all of God's actions is His deep desire to redeem all sinners, but He can't do that unless those sinners repent (Isaiah 59:1-2; 2 Peter 3:9). By delivering Jonah from death and disobedience and sending him to Nineveh, God demonstrated His willingness to forgive all who repent—the people of Nineveh, Jonah himself, and the rebellious Israelites. In short, Jonah's story reveals "God's all-sovereign power and care."[50]

"Sovereign" is not a word to be used lightly. It means "above or superior to all others; supreme in power, rank, or authority." In human history, it is generally used to describe a king or ruler who has absolute power. In the purest sense of the word, it should apply only to God.

How do we know God is sovereign? Because He is superior or supreme in

- authority and power, dominant in every element of existence;

- quality and performance, incapable of making a mistake;

- degree—the utmost, the ultimate, the highest of the high—the original and final Source;

- rulership of creation, controlling all natural elements;

- essence—not limited or affected by time, space, or physical conditions;

- presence—always everywhere, eternally;

---

50   Ellison 363.

- knowledge and wisdom, always aware of everything.

God reveals His sovereignty *to* and *through* Jonah, physically and spiritually, delivering him *from* death and *to* obedience, *to* preaching, and *to* a greater understanding of God's character. God patiently teaches Jonah about compassion by caring for him, even as he pouts and complains (Jonah 4:10-11).

Application: Are We like Jonah?

People today are really not very different from the people in Jonah's day. We are caught up in living our lives according to whatever standards we learned from our parents and our culture. Those who do not know God worship false religious doctrines created by men or idols such as money, power, pleasure, or success. Those who do know God have in their hearts the desire to live by His words and to tell others His wonderful message—the very message that Jonah used as the conclusion to his song: "Salvation is of the Lord" (2:9).

God has always gone to great lengths to draw men and women out of sin (John 3:16; 2 Peter 3:9). He has demonstrated time and again His willingness to move heaven and earth to reach lost souls. For Jonah, He went to the bottom of the ocean. For pagans long ago, He went to Nineveh. For rebellious Israel and Judah, He spoke through prophets. For the whole world—even the world of today—He went to the cross.

As followers of Christ, are we willing to submit to God's sovereignty and make His purpose our purpose? Most of us can quote Matthew 28:18-20 and Mark 16:15-16. We may be less familiar with Luke's record of this Great Commission:

> Then He said to them, "Thus it is written, and thus it was necessary for the Christ
> to suffer and to rise from the dead the third day,[47] and that repentance and remission
> of sins should be preached in His name to all nations, beginning at Jerusalem"
> (Luke 24:46-47).

If it was "necessary" for Christ to suffer and to rise from the dead—and it was—then the preaching of repentance and remission of sins is also necessary. Surely most of us would agree that the mission of the Lord's Church today is still to preach the gospel, to baptize, and to teach new Christians to live faithful lives.

As we pursue that goal, we can learn from Jonah. We must never allow prejudice, fear, disobedience, lack of compassion, or the lack of knowledge of God to hinder the teaching of His extraordinary message: through Christ, the Sovereign Lord God still offers salvation—deliverance—from sin today. It is free to everyone who is willing to receive it by obedience.

Just Thinking . . .

1. Discuss comments concerning Jonah and Nineveh made by Jesus in Matthew 12:38-45 and Luke 11:29-32.

2. How do Christians today sometimes resemble Jonah? What hinders us from sharing the gospel with the people around us?

3. Find examples of God's sovereignty in the Bible. Begin with Jonah's song; how does it illustrate God's authority and power? Consider also Genesis 1; John 1:1-3; Isaiah 55:8-9; Exodus 3:6,13-15; and Luke 20:37.

Chapter 9

Deliverance in Captivity

Daniel 1-3

Captive Heroes

Besieged! Jerusalem's walls couldn't stand much longer; the Babylonian soldiers would attack again soon. Inside the city, some begged God to deliver them; others cursed Him, as they had cursed God's prophets who warned that He would no longer tolerate apostasy. Their wicked king, faithless priests, and unrepentant citizens had incurred God's wrath; now everyone would suffer.

When the walls fell, Daniel, Hananiah, Mishael, and Azariah were taken as captives to Babylon. They found themselves not in chains but in training. King Nebuchadnezzar expected them to learn the language and literature of the Chaldeans and Babylonians; then they would serve him.

Ashpenaz, their trainer, assigned them Babylonian names: Belteshazzar, Shadrach, Meshach, and Abed-Nego. *First our names, then our religion,* thought Daniel.[51] Next, Ashpenaz brought them meat and wine. "From the king's table," he boasted. "See how he honors you!"

Daniel had purposed in his heart not to defile himself with unclean meat or food offered to idols, but when he tried to explain, the steward said, "I fear the king; if you look underfed, I could lose my head!"

"Test us," suggested Daniel. "Bring us vegetables and water for ten days. Then compare us to those who are eating the king's delicacies and treat us according to our appearance." Reluctantly, Ashpenaz complied. Ten days later, these four men looked healthier than all the others.

After three years of study, they had an interview with King Nebuchadnezzar; he found them to be ten times wiser than all his astrologers and magicians. God had given them healthy bodies and skillful minds, and to Daniel He also gave the ability to understand dreams and visions. Thus, Daniel, Shadrach, Meshach, and Abed-Nego entered the service of King Nebuchadnezzar.[52] (Based on 2 Chronicles 36:10-18; Daniel 1).

Tested

Daniel was a prisoner; why did he risk challenging Ashpenaz over food? Though devout Jews were serious about obeying the food laws, Daniel could have reasoned that God wouldn't expect him to obey them when he had no control over the food he received.

Instead, Daniel chose to make an effort. He didn't go on a hunger strike or try to escape. He understood the steward's position and made a reasonable request that protected Ashpenaz. God helped Daniel find favor with his captors, and Daniel resolved to maintain his godly character. Think about the elements at work:

- God was in control: He allowed the captivity, then used it.

---

51   Gleason L. Archer, Jr., "Daniel" in *Daniel and the Minor Prophets,* The Expositor's Bible Commentary, ed. Frank E. Gaebelein, vol. 7 (Grand Rapids, Mich.: Zondervan, 1985) 34. Their Hebrew names referenced God; their Babylonian names referenced Babylonian idols.

52   The Book of Daniel uses both Hebrew and Babylonian names for the four Hebrew men. After noting the name change, I used the names Daniel, Shadrach, Meshach, and Abed-Nego as these seem more familiar.

- Daniel trusted God to help him do what was right.

- God equipped the four young men to meet the challenges of captivity.

- The young men realized God had a purpose for them and determined to learn so they could be worthy witnesses to God's work.

Just Thinking . . .

1. Daniel "purposed in his heart" to avoid defilement. What does that mean? In what ways can we as Christians avoid defilement from the sinful world around us?

2. Though we are not bound by laws about clean and unclean food today as the Jews were, are there certain foods and drinks that Christians should avoid? Why or why not?

A Reason to Praise

Having graduated with honors, Daniel, Shadrach, Meshach, and Abed-Nego were given jobs within King Nebuchadnezzar's administration. God delivered them *from* the threat of death and *to* lives of privilege and importance. However, deliverance brings responsibility, and privilege doesn't always protect; even godly people may be tempted or betrayed.

Daniel 2 reports that Nebuchadnezzar had a troubling dream. He summoned his magicians, astrologers, and other trusted advisors and demanded that they tell him the dream and its interpretation. (This unreasonable request suggests the possibility that the king remembered the disturbing nature of the dream but not the dream itself).When they said that only the gods could do such a thing, he condemned them all to death.

Arioch, captain of the king's guard, immediately began to carry out the decree. When he knocked on Daniel's door, Daniel answered Arioch "with counsel and wisdom," asking, "Why is the decree from the king so urgent?" (Daniel 2:14-15). When Arioch explained, Daniel went to the king and calmly requested time to discover the information.

Daniel didn't know the dream, but he knew that God knows everything. Daniel enlisted his three friends to "seek mercies from the God of heaven concerning this secret," (vv. 17-18). Archer calls this group effort "a concert of prayer," implying that when God's people unite in prayer, the sound is sweet in God's ear and great things happen.[53] Daniel displays "God-confidence" as opposed to self-confidence. Perhaps he remembered Joseph, Israel's well-known dreamer and interpreter, and so Daniel trusted God.

When God reveals the secret in a night vision, Daniel is filled with wonder and an even greater grasp of God's power and purpose. He "blessed the name of God" with words that could be called a prayer or a song of praise and thanksgiving. By giving Daniel the information the king demanded, God delivers Daniel, his friends, and all the magicians and advisors. Daniel is so sure of God's deliverance, he pauses to express his gratitude to God *before* reporting to King Nebuchadnezzar.

The Song

Daniel records his joyous delight with God's answer by blessing or praising God's name and illustrating two of God's greatest attributes.

> [20] Daniel answered and said:
>
> 'Blessed be the **name of God** forever and ever,
> For **wisdom and might** are His.

---

53   Archer 43.

²¹ And He changes the times and the seasons;
He **removes kings** and **raises up kings;**
He **gives wisdom** to the wise
And **knowledge** to those who have understanding.
²² He reveals deep and secret things;
He knows what *is* in the darkness,
And **light dwells** with Him.

Because He possesses wisdom and might and shares them with "those who have understanding," God deserves to be blessed or praised "forever and ever." Daniel had learned wisdom during his training, which can be defined as combining knowledge gained by discernment with the correct application of knowledge. It also involves "living responsibly before God and coping successfully with every problem or task confronting him as a servant of God."[54] The king had asked the impossible of his magicians and advisors; Daniel was wise enough to know that only God could provide the answer.

Verse 21 relates directly to the king's dream. God shows King Nebuchadnezzar a series of kingdoms that will come after him, "removing" and "raising up kings," but he needs Daniel, a man of God, to explain the dream. In this way, God honors the king by giving him knowledge but also tells him that God is in control and that man's knowledge is incomplete without God's explanation.

Verse 22 notes that man can't know "deep and secret things" without revelation from God. Man looks at darkness and wonders what is hidden there; God knows, for light dwells with Him. "Light" is a quality attributed to God and Jesus throughout the Bible (Psalm 119:105; John 8:12; 1 John 1:5).

²³ I **thank** You and **praise** You,
O God of my fathers;
You have given me **wisdom and might,**
And have now **made known to me what we asked** of You,
For You have made known to us the king's demand.

God's "might" or power is unlimited, and His wisdom is unparalleled in the world. Daniel claims no discernment or ability to understand the dream. He freely credits God with giving him wisdom and might as well as making known "what we asked of You," recognizing the answer to collective prayer.

Just Thinking . . .

1. Though not called a song, how does this passage resemble songs we have studied?

2. How is it different?

The Revelation

After thanking God, Daniel goes first to Arioch to stop the executions, then to the king (Daniel 2:24-25). Nebuchadnezzar wastes no time: "Are you able to make known to me the dream which I have seen, and its interpretation?" (v. 26).

Daniel explains that no man can answer him, "But there is a God in heaven who reveals secrets" (v. 28). With humility, Daniel states that God wants the king to know the secrets of the future (vv. verses 29-30). Daniel recounts both the dream and its meaning, which is no less than a preview of future kingdoms.

Verses 31-35 describe a great statue with a head of gold, chest and arms of silver, belly and thighs of

---

54   Archer 38.

bronze, legs of iron, and feet of iron and clay. A stone not cut with hands strikes the statue and destroys it, leaving no trace, but the stone becomes a great mountain, filling the earth.

The head of gold is Nebuchadnezzar; Daniel emphasizes that God gave him this great kingdom of Babylon. The other parts of the statue represent succeeding inferior kingdoms, generally accepted as the Medes and Persians, the Greeks, and the Romans. The feet of iron and clay symbolize both the strength and weakness of the Roman kingdom; during this time period, a kingdom not made with hands would "break in pieces and consume all these kingdoms, and it shall stand forever" (vv. verses 42-44).

Overwhelmed, the king falls on his face before Daniel, acknowledging God: "Truly your God is the God of gods, the Lord of kings, and a revealer of secrets, since you could reveal this secret" (v. 47). Daniel receives gifts and becomes ruler of Babylon and chief administrator of the advisors and wise men. At Daniel's request, the king also appoints Shadrach, Meshach, and Abed-Nego as administrators.

Daniel delivers and is delivered. By God's counsel, he rescues the king's advisors, including himself and his companions, from death, and opens the eyes and heart of a powerful pagan king to the only true and living God and to the transience of human governments.

Just Thinking . . .

1. What were Daniel and his companions delivered from? What were they delivered to?

2. Everyone has a sphere of influence—people whose lives are touched by our words and actions. Who were the people in Daniel's sphere of influence? Who are the people in yours? How can you influence people for good?

Unsung Deliverance from Persecution

While King Nebuchadnezzar was properly impressed with God as "a revealer of secrets," his confession of God as "the God of gods, the Lord of kings" had little effect on religious life in Babylon. The king didn't convert to Judaism, and it soon became clear that he didn't grasp the finer implications of the revelation. In particular, he didn't understand monotheism, the worship of one god; if asked, he would probably would have called it silly or even dangerous.

Worshiping multiple gods was normal, so the addition of a new image wouldn't bother most people. Perhaps inspired by his dream, Nebuchadnezzar ordered the building of a gold image 90 feet tall and 9 feet wide; he placed it on the plain of Dura (3:1). Then he ordered everyone in his government to attend the dedication ceremony. He assembled an orchestra and issued a command: When the music played, everyone had to "fall down and worship the gold image" (v. 5). Anyone who did not obey would be thrown immediately into a burning fiery furnace (v. 6).

Why?

Babylonians didn't practice emperor worship, so this image probably wasn't a likeness of Nebuchadnezzar, but it may have been an image of Nebo, also called Nabu, the Babylonian god of the art of writing and vegetation.[55] However, since his name was part of the king's name, he was probably the king's patron god, and loyalty to Nebo translated as loyalty to the king.[56]

Why did he order the death penalty for failure to comply? Powerful leaders want control; they don't tolerate dissent. A terrifying threat should prevent disobedience; who would dare risk the king's wrath? And who would tell the king if someone did disobey?

---

55   *Encyclopedia Britannica,* "Nabu," online at http://www.britannica.com/EBchecked/topic/401331/Nabu
56   Archer 50-51.

70

Tattletales

Who, indeed? The king favored Daniel, Shadrach, Meshach, and Abed-Nego, promoting them to positions of importance and possibly displacing earlier favorites. Also, some would have disapproved based on race. The Chaldeans considered themselves ethnically superior to Jews.[57] If they resented the king's policy of educating and rewarding Jewish captives, this show of disrespect by the men he had promoted was a perfect "I-told-you-so" moment.

Dedication Day arrived. The crowd gathered; music sounded. All the people touched their noses to the ground before the image—except Shadrach, Meshach, and Abed-Nego. They stood. Full of righteous indignation, the Chaldeans tattled (3:8-12).

"Is It True?"

Nebuchadnezzar was furious. How could they flaunt his authority, after all he had done for them? He summoned the three men and asked, "Is it true? Do you refuse to worship the gold image?" (v. 14). He seemed genuinely shocked, but before they could reply, he offered them a second chance: "If . . . you fall down and worship the image which I have made, good! But if you do not worship, you shall be cast immediately into the midst of a burning fiery furnace. And who is the god who will deliver you from my hands?" (v.15).

Nebuchadnezzar's benevolent offer was tarnished by the arrogance of the last sentence. He insulted God by equating Him with man-made idols and implying no god could save those whom the mighty Nebuchadnezzar had condemned!

Just Thinking . . .

1. What possible motives prompted King Nebuchadnezzar to build the gold image and order everyone to worship it? What were the possible motives of the "tattletales?"

2. Why was King Nebuchadnezzar so angry when the three men refused to worship the idol? Why did he give them a second chance to obey him?

"But if Not . . ."

Having experienced God's deliverance at least four times since becoming captives, we shouldn't be surprised that Shadrach, Meshach, and Abed-Nego stood firm in their faith.[58] They answered with remarkable faith:

> [16] . . . O Nebuchadnezzar, we have no need to answer you in this matter.
> [17] If that is the case, our God whom we serve **is able to deliver us** from the burning fiery furnace, and He will deliver us from your hand, O king.
> [18] **But if not**, let it be known to you, O king, that **we do not serve your gods, nor will we worship the gold image** which you have set up (3:16-18).

Verse 16 implies the king should know the answer. Archer suggests that a more appropriate translation of verse 17 is, "If our God exists, whom we worship, he is able to deliver us from the furnace of burning fire, and from your hand, O king, he shall deliver."[59]

---

57   Archer 83.
58   They escaped death in Jerusalem, prospered from a God-approved diet, succeeded in their training, and escaped death again when Daniel described and explained the king's dream.
59   Archer 54.

Verse 18 should amaze us: Shadrach, Meshach and Abed-Nego prefer death over idol worship! They know God *can* deliver them; they know he *will* deliver them—either by miraculous intervention or by bringing them home to Himself. If His will is better served by their death, they are ready to die.

When the choice is death or disobedience to God, death is deliverance.

The Fiery Furnace

Enraged, the king increases the heat in the furnace seven times hotter than normal and orders the victims to be bound hand and foot and fully clothed. He sacrifices "certain mighty men of valor" who die when they throw the captives into the super-heated furnace. Shadrach, Meshach, and Abed-Nego "fell down bound into the midst of the burning fiery furnace" (v. 23).

Watching from a safe distance, King Nebuchadnezzar expects the men to disintegrate almost instantly, but they don't. In astonishment, the king asks, "Didn't we cast three men bound into the fire? I see four men loose and walking around—and the fourth is like the Son of God!" The king calls the "servants of the Most High God" out of the flames. The fourth figure disappears, but Shadrach, Meshach, and Abed-Nego step out of the furnace completely unharmed (vv. verses 24-27).

The king can't deny the miracle, the reward of faith, or the supreme power of the God of Israel. He blesses God and curses anyone who speaks against Him because "there is no other God who can deliver like this" (vv. verses 28-29). He also promotes the three men who survive the trial by fire.

The Bible doesn't include a song of deliverance from Shadrach, Meshach, and Abed-Nego, and they are not mentioned again, though Hebrews 11:32-34 alludes to them. If these three men were familiar with David's songs, they might have agreed that Psalm 5:11-12 contains a few lines worthy of the occasion:

> [11]But let all those rejoice who put their trust in You;
> Let them ever shout for joy, because You defend them;
> Let those also who love Your name
> Be joyful in You.
> [12] For You, O LORD, will bless the righteous;
> With favor You will surround him as with a shield.

Application: "It Can't Happen Here!"

Most American Christians have never experienced persecution for their religious beliefs. Most may think they never will because the United States Constitution protects "freedom of religion." Yet without researching the issue, I can name disturbing changes that have taken place in the last 50 years. I'm 62 now; when I was a child, we

- prayed and read the Bible in school;

- sang "God Bless America" and other hymns in school;

- didn't object to "one nation under God" when we said the Pledge of Allegiance;

- talked about God and church naturally and without censor;

- didn't study evolution as "fact;"

- received a free "Gideon" New Testament in fifth grade.

Such activities in public schools today would reap suspension and/or a lawsuit.

A brief review of world news reveals that Christians are routinely restricted, persecuted, and even killed in places like Egypt, China, and North Korea. "It can't happen here" is a poor defense against persecution, especially in light of 2 Timothy 3:12: "Yes, and all who desire to live godly in Christ Jesus will suffer persecution."

In the short term, Daniel and his friends might have justified eating the king's food, but that would have made it easier to give in to the next restriction, and the next. Instead, they stood firm and God delivered them.

If we as Christians found ourselves subject to a non-Christian ruler, would we obey laws that prohibited meeting with the church or praying with our family and friends? Would we publically renounce Christ by "bowing" to government edicts?

And if it should come to us, if someone with a gun or an army or a bomb tells us to renounce our Lord, will we comply? Or will we say, "Our God will deliver us, *but even if He doesn't*, we will not renounce Christ, for He died for us"?

After all, what's the worst thing they could do—send us to Paradise?

> **Just Thinking . . .**
>
> 1. Read aloud the answer that Shadrach, Meshach and Abed-Nego gave the king in Daniel 3:16-18. What was the source of their courage? List Scriptures to support your answer.
>
> 2. Many governments today forbid Christians to meet openly or to evangelize. What qualities do Christians need to develop in order to withstand persecution?

Chapter 10

The Song of Mary

The Song of the Heavenly Host

The Song of Simeon

Luke 1:46-55; 2:8-8; 2:25-35

Young Woman of God

She was probably doing something ordinary, like washing dishes or sweeping. Perhaps she was day-dreaming about Joseph and their wedding plans. She looked up from her work and saw someone—a man? He spoke: "Rejoice, highly favored one, the Lord is with you; blessed are you among women!"

What a strange greeting! What could it mean? He sensed her troubled reaction and reassured her, "Do not be afraid, Mary, for you have found favor with God. And behold, you will conceive in your womb and bring forth a Son, and shall call His name Jesus. He will be great, and will be called the Son of the Highest; and the Lord God will give Him the throne of His father David. And He will reign over the house of Jacob forever, and of His kingdom there will be no end."

Such amazing words! She scarcely knew what to say, but one question seemed most important. "How can this be, since I do not know a man?"

The angel explained that the Holy Spirit would overshadow her with power from the Highest. "The Holy One who is to be born will be called the Son of God." He also told Mary that her barren relative Elizabeth was six months pregnant. "For with God nothing will be impossible."

Mary bowed her head and said, "Behold the maidservant of the Lord! Let it be to me according to your word." When she looked up the angel was gone, but her ears tingled as she recalled his words.

A baby! But not just any baby—The Son of God, a king on David's throne—that meant—no it couldn't be—but what else could it mean? She breathed the word, the hope of Israel: *Messiah!* Could it be true?

She felt joyful and frightened all at once. "I must tell Joseph—no, my mother. But—what if they don't believe me?" A betrothal was as binding as a marriage vow. If she were found with child before the wedding, everyone would think—she blushed. Remembering the angel's words, she knew who would understand.

* * *

Mary approached the home of her kinswoman. She opened the door and stepped inside, calling, "Elizabeth? It's Mary. I bring you greetings from our family."

An older woman looked up. With one hand on her rounded belly, she smiled at her young relative; then she placed her other hand on Mary's belly. "Blessed are you among women, and blessed is the fruit of your womb! But why is this granted to me, that the mother of my Lord should come to me? For indeed, as soon as the voice of your greeting sounded in my ears, the babe leaped in my womb for joy."

Mary tried to speak, but Elizabeth continued, "Blessed is she who believed, for there will be a fulfillment of those things which were told her from the Lord." The two women hugged; then Mary began to sing. (Based on Luke 1:26-45).

Ordinary People

God often works His extraordinary will through ordinary people who submit and serve Him. When it was time to send Jesus to the earth, God worked through two faithful couples who rejoiced in the blessing of God's eternal plan: Mary and Joseph and Zacharias and Elizabeth. We will focus on songs about the birth of Jesus in this chapter and consider the Song of Zacharias in the next chapter.

God's promise to send a Redeemer reverberates throughout the Old Testament in prophetic anticipation. By New Testament times, when the Jews suffered under Roman rule, 42 generations had waited for that promise to be fulfilled (Matthew 1:17). Many longed for Him; few could have imagined the humble manner of His coming.

Elizabeth's greeting confirms everything Gabriel had told Mary, and she grasps the beauty and truth of her situation: She is to be the mother of Messiah! Amazement and gratitude replace her worries, and she praises God in song.

The Song of Mary

Mary's song echoes Hannah's in attitude and imagery; it also borrows from the Psalms. These similarities don't diminish her jubilant praise; in fact, they point to the rich literary heritage of the Jews and highlight Mary's knowledge of it. Even a poor Jewish girl from Nazareth with little formal education could have memorized songs and prophecies from synagogue and temple services. Mary also adds touches of her own.

In addition, the Holy Spirit, mentioned several times in Luke 1 and 2, surely inspired Mary's words since all Scripture is God-breathed (Luke 1:35, 41, 67, 80; 2:25-27).

Mary's song in Luke 1:46-55 consists of four parts with overlapping themes: praise for God's kindness, attributes of God, sovereignty of God, and God's mercy for Israel. [60]

> [46] And Mary said:
>
> 'My soul **magnifies** the Lord,
> [47] And my spirit **has rejoiced** in God my Savior.
> [48] For He has **regarded the lowly state** of His maidservant;
> For behold, henceforth all generations will **call me blessed.**

Mary no doubt grew up believing in God's greatness and power, but her encounter with Gabriel has "magnified" or "enlarged" her perception of God. He is even greater than she imagined, taking notice of a lowly maidservant who acknowledges her own need for the Savior (v. 47). Future generations will know how God blessed her.

In verse 49, she praises God for the "great things" He has done for her.

> [49] For He who is **mighty** has done great things for me,
> And **holy** *is* His name.
> [50] And His **mercy** *is* on those who fear Him
> From generation to generation.

60   Walter L. Liefeld, "Luke," in *Matthew, Mark, Luke,* The Expositor's Bible Commentary, ed. Frank E. Gaebelein, vol. 8 (Grand Rapids, Mich.: Zondervan, 1984) 835.

Rather than list God's actions, Mary focuses on His attributes: mighty (power), holy name, and mercy. In the Old Testament, "mighty" often carries the image of a warrior who defeats all enemies, suggesting extraordinary strength. "And holy is His name" illustrates that a person's name represents one's character, reputation, and authority. To Mary, God is holy in every way. "Mercy" is a gift of grace for those who "fear" or "show reverence" to God.

> [51] He has shown **strength** with His arm;
> He has **scattered the proud** in the imagination of their hearts.
> [52] He has **put down the mighty** from their thrones,
> And **exalted the lowly.**
> [53] He has **filled the hungry** with good things,
> And the **rich He has sent away empty.**

Verses 51-53 give examples of God's great strength, including role reversals of the proud and lowly as well as the hungry and the rich. God is sovereign; when He acts, dramatic changes take place. Like Hannah, Mary sees the difference between man's apparent strength and God's real strength; the proud think they are strong, but God will scatter and remove them from power while exalting the weak.

> [54] He **has helped** His servant Israel,
> In remembrance of His **mercy,**
> [55] As He spoke to our fathers,
> To Abraham and to his seed forever.'

In the last four lines, Mary suggests that as God has helped Israel in the past, He will help in the future—in fact, forever! God promised to bless "all the nations of the earth" through Abraham's seed (Genesis 22:18). Mary understands that the Child in her womb is the Seed of Abraham—God's Messiah—though she doesn't grasp all the implications of His coming.

Mary stays with Elizabeth "about three months." At home she faces Joseph and her family. Joseph wanted to "put her away secretly" to avoid public shame. However, God reassures him by sending an angel in a dream to explain that the Child was conceived through the Holy Spirit to fulfill Isaiah 7:14. So Joseph marries her (Matthew 1:18-23).

When Caesar Augustus decrees that the Jews should be registered in the cities of their ancestors, Mary and Joseph go to Bethlehem, David's city. While there, ". . . she brought forth her firstborn Son, and wrapped Him in swaddling cloths, and laid Him in a manger, because there was no room for them in the inn" (Luke 2:6-7). In this quiet, humble way, Messiah was born.

Just Thinking . . .

1. Consider the similarities and differences of Mary's song and Hannah's. How are the two women alike and different? What verse in Hannah's song contains a prophecy about Messiah?

2. A doctrine called "Immaculate Conception" states that Mary was free of sin, or she could not have had the sinless Child, Jesus. How does the use of "God my Savior" in verse 47 contradict this doctrine?

The Song of the Heavenly Host

The announcement of His birth, however, was anything but quiet or humble. Not far from Bethlehem, shepherds watching their flock at night were the first to hear the announcement of the Savior's birth:

> [9] And behold, an angel of the Lord stood before them, and the glory of the Lord shone around them, and they were greatly afraid. Then the angel said to them, 'Do not be afraid, for behold, I bring you good tidings of great joy which will be to all people. [11] For there is born to you this day in the city of David a Savior, who is Christ the Lord . . . .You will find a Babe wrapped in swaddling cloths, lying in a manger' (2:9-12).

Messiah had come! Every generation anticipated this announcement; everyone hoped to see God's Anointed. Why was this dramatic, world-changing event announced first to shepherds? After all, people at this time considered shepherds untrustworthy and ceremonially unclean.[61] When God promised to establish David's throne forever, He said, "I took you from the sheepfold" to rule Israel—an impressive promotion (2 Samuel 7:8). Perhaps God wanted to emphasize that the first to hear the gospel were social outcasts, especially since Jesus would be criticized for associating with "sinners."[62]

Yet God also uses the name "shepherds" to symbolize those who lead His people in both the Old and New Testaments (Psalm 23:1; Isaiah 40:11; Jeremiah 23:1-4; Hebrews 13:20; 1 Peter 2:25; 5:2). Who better than shepherds could welcome the Good Shepherd? (John 10: 11-15).

Reassured by the angel's words, the shepherds now listen to praise from heaven:

> [13] And suddenly there was with the angel a multitude of the heavenly host **praising God** and saying:
>
> [14] '**Glory to God** in the highest,
> And on **earth peace, goodwill** toward men!'

"Multitude" suggests hundreds or even thousands; "heavenly host" suggests a band or army of heavenly bodies or angels. Their brief praise captures the essence of God's relationship with mankind. God is "the highest" in the highest place physically (in heaven) and spiritually (Creator) in relationship to His people—the One Moses called "gloriously glorious."

Messiah has come to restore peace between God and mankind—peace broken by sin long ago in Eden. When Jesus enters Jerusalem riding on a colt just a few days before His death, a multitude of disciples rejoice, connecting this event with an Old Testament refrain and the message from the angels: "'Blessed is the King who comes in the name of the LORD!' Peace in heaven and glory in the highest!" (Luke 19:37-38; cf. Psalm 118:26).

Liefeld notes that "goodwill toward men" is better translated as "and on earth peace to men on whom his favor rests."[63] While God intends goodwill to all, only those who obediently and faithfully accept the grace or favor Messiah provides will know His peace, for only His sacrifice can deliver it (John 14:6).

The angels return to heaven; the shepherds "make haste" to Bethlehem and find Mary and Joseph. They see the Babe in the manger and become the first evangelists, telling the good news of the Savior's birth. All who heard "marveled;" the shepherds return to their flocks, "glorifying and praising God" for all they had heard and seen. Mary, however, "kept all these things and pondered them in her heart" (Luke 2:16-20).

---

61   Liefeld 845.

62   Liefeld 845.

63   Liefeld 846.

Just Thinking . . .

1. Luke doesn't say that the angels sang; he says they praised God. Throughout the Book of Psalms, the words "praise" and "song" are often closely associated, as in Psalms 28:7; 40:3; 69:30; and 98:1. Is it possible to praise without singing? Why or why not?

2. Shepherds were the first to see Jesus (except for His parents). What does this suggest about the kind of people who would be most receptive to Christ?

3. What did the shepherds do after they saw Jesus? What characteristics of shepherds make them good examples for leaders?

The Song of Simeon

Luke 2:29-32

Mary and Joseph go to Jerusalem and present Jesus to the Lord; they also offer a sacrifice of two turtle-doves or young pigeons, testifying to their poverty (Exodus 13:2; Leviticus 12:7-8).

In the temple, a man named Simeon approaches them. Luke describes Simeon as a just and devout man who was waiting for "the Consolation of Israel." God had promised he would not die until he had seen "the Lord's Christ" (Luke 2:25-26). He takes the baby in his arms and blesses God.

> [29] Lord, now You are letting Your servant depart in peace,
> According to Your word;
> [30] For my eyes **have seen Your salvation**
> [31] Which You have prepared before the face of all peoples,
> [32] A **light to bring revelation to the Gentiles,**
> And the glory of Your people Israel.

This brief statement has the form of a poem or song with three sets of contrasting parallel statements. "Lord" contrasts with "your servant," Simeon, who can die in peace since God has fulfilled His promise. We don't know his age, but this moment is clearly the high point of his life. "For my eyes have seen Your salvation" contrasts with "prepared before the face of all peoples." He has seen salvation embodied, but everyone will have the opportunity to share this gift from God (Isaiah 52:10; Psalm 98:3).

Verse 32 contrasts "Gentiles" with "Your people Israel." Simeon correctly interprets Isaiah 49:6: One "light" (Jesus) reveals salvation to the Gentiles and glorifies Israel. This thought is similar to Luke 1:78-79 at the end of the Song of Zacharias.

Witnessing the coming of Messiah fills Simeon with wonder and awe, so he declares God's deliverance. Simeon is delivered *from* waiting—no small gift when we remember how many faithful prophets longed to see God's promise fulfilled (Hebrews 11:39; 1 Peter 1:10-13). He is delivered *to* praise, blessing, and prophecy.

Mary and Joseph are amazed at Simeon's message, which was probably heard by many of the people preset in the temple. Then he speaks to Mary more privately, blessing them but also including a warning: Jesus' destiny will change the world with the opportunity for salvation, but to some He will be a stumbling block, and a sword will pierce Mary's soul as well (Luke 2:34-35; cf. Isaiah 8:14-15).

In addition, a prophetess and widow named Anna who had served in the temple most of her long life sees Jesus and thanks the Lord. Though no song is recorded for Anna, she clearly recognizes the Savior; Luke records that she "spoke of Him to all those who looked for redemption in Jerusalem" (2:36-38).

1. There must have been thousands of Jews who hoped to live long enough to see Messiah, yet the Bible records only a few who saw and knew Him as an infant. Why Simeon? Why Anna?

2. Besides the blessing for them, what purpose was served by Simeon's and Anna's encounter with Jesus and His parents?

Application: Accepting God's Purpose

Of all the people who participated in the pivotal moment in history when God came in the flesh, Mary probably fascinates us the most. Some worship her; others deny the virgin birth. From the Bible account of her life, Mary demonstrated at least three character traits that made her a good mother for Jesus.

Submission: "Behold the maidservant of the Lord! Let it be to me according to your word" (Luke 1:38). Mary didn't understand the how or why of Gabriel's message, but she submitted to God's will. Too often, when we don't understand the commands God has given us, we try to modify them to suit our purpose. Mary submitted.

Faith: Gabriel told Mary, "For with God nothing will be impossible" (Luke 1:37). God's mission for Mary complicated her life: unwed pregnancy; travel to Bethlehem and later Egypt; rearing a Child whose purpose in life is unique; suffering because of His suffering. Mary trusted God and walked by faith.

Contemplation: Mary's song "magnifies" God for what He accomplished through her, not what she accomplished. Her reaction to the praise for her baby is to keep her thoughts and questions to herself and to "ponder" them (Luke 2:19,33). Mary didn't boast about her status as Messiah's mother or speculate about His mission. She did more thinking than speaking, a habit that would benefit most of us.

Just Thinking . . .

1. Mary's song illustrates God's strength as He reverses the positions of the proud and rich while exalting the lowly and hungry. How does the gospel of Christ affect social status and position? Consider Galatians 3:27-29 and Colossians 3:10-13.

2. From the little we know of Mary's personality, what do you think qualified her to rear the Son of God?

Chapter 11
The Song of Zacharias
Luke 1:67-79

Zacharias and Elizabeth

At the hour of incense, worshipers came to the temple to pray. Inside, Zacharias prepared his censer and turned his mind to prayer. He and his wife Elizabeth were righteous people, committed to keeping God's Law. Their one srrow was that they were childless. Though they were were old now, Zacharias still prayed about his wife's barrenness.

He approached the altar with the censer and was startled to see someone standing beside it on the right side. Strange—only the priest chosen by lot to offer incense should be here. Then the angel spoke:

> Do not be afraid, Zacharias, for your prayer is heard; and your wife Elizabeth will bear you a son, and you shall call his name John. [14] And you will have joy and gladness, and many will rejoice at his birth. [15] For he will be great in the sight of the Lord, and shall drink neither wine nor strong drink. He will also be filled with the Holy Spirit, even from his mother's womb. [16] And he will turn many of the children of Israel to the Lord their God. [17] He will also go before Him in the spirit and power of Elijah, 'to turn the hearts of the fathers to the children,' and the disobedient to the wisdom of the just, to make ready a people prepared for the Lord (Luke 1:13-17; Malachi 4:5-6).

Stunned, Zacharias answered this most unreasonable announcement with reason: "How shall I know this? I am an old man, and my wife is well advanced in years."

"I am Gabriel, who stands in God's presence. I was sent to bring you glad tidings. Since you don't believe me, you will be mute until these words are fulfilled in their own time." Then he was gone.

Trembling, Zacharias touched the censer to the incense; he opened his mouth to pray and tasted silent air. He walked outside, unable to offer a blessing to the waiting worshipers.

"What is wrong with the priest?"

"Has he seen a vision?"

"What can it mean?" Murmurs ran through the crowd, but Zacharias could only gesture. When his time of service ended, he went home. Soon–wonder of wonders–Elizabeth was pregnant! For five months, she and her silent husband kept to themselves, rejoicing quietly at God's generosity. Then in her sixth month, Elizabeth had a visitor.

When she saw her relative, Elizabeth was filled with the Holy Spirit. She greeted Mary with words that confirmed Zacharias' experience as well as Mary's. The baby in Elizabeth's womb leaped for joy at Mary's greeting. As Mary praised God, she and Elizabeth knew they were part of something bigger than they had ever imagined.

Zacharias knew it as well, but he couldn't speak. Only after his son was born, only after he obeyed Gabriel's command to name the baby "John," was Zacharias able to proclaim the promise–the Good News–that

Messiah was coming, and his son John would go before Him. (Based on Luke 1:5-25, 39-45, 57-64).

Just Thinking . . .

1. Zacharias and Mary each ask Gabriel a question when he reveals his remarkable news in Luke 1:13-20 and 1:30-37. Zacharias is made mute because he didn't believe Gabriel, but Mary is not reprimanded. What is the difference between their questions?

2. How are Elizabeth and Hannah alike? How are they different?

Another Ordinary Family

Luke interweaves the story of Mary, Joseph, and the birth of Jesus with the story of another ordinary family, Zacharias and Elizabeth, and the birth of their son John. As we noted in the last chapter, Mary visited Elizabeth and stayed about three months. Soon after Mary returned home, Elizabeth delivered her baby boy.

The birth created quite a stir; neighbors and relatives rejoiced over the great mercy God had bestowed on Elizabeth, perhaps recalling other barren women who became mothers in Israelite history. At the baby's circumcision, everyone assumed he would be named after his father, but Elizabeth insisted on calling him "John." When consulted, Zacharias wrote, "His name is John." Only then could Zacharias speak, "praising God" (v. 64).

"Then fear came on all who dwelt around them; and all these sayings were discussed throughout all the hill country of Judea" (v. 65), suggesting that Zacharias either described his encounter with Gabriel or launched directly into his song. Those present wondered about John's future as his father revealed information about Messiah.

The Song of Zacharias

Luke 1:67-70

Part 1

Luke writes that Zacharias "was filled with the Holy Spirit, and prophesied" (v. 67). The song has two parts unified by a poetic device called "chiasmus," or inverted parallelism.[64] Key words or their synonyms from the first part of the song are repeated in reverse order in the second part. Notice the use of "visited," "people," "salvation," "prophet," "enemies," "fathers" and "covenant" in verses 68-75, Part 1, which focus on praise for God's messianic deliverance.

In verse 73, "oath" echoes "covenant" and begins the reverse order that moves into Part 2, which celebrates John's important role in that great work (verses 76-79): "father," "enemies," "prophet," "salvation," "people," and "visited."

> [68] Blessed *is* the Lord God of Israel,
> For He has **visited** and redeemed His **people,**
> [69] And has raised up a horn of **salvation** for us
> In the house of His servant David,
> [70] As He spoke by the mouth of His holy **prophets,**
> Who have been since the world began,
>
> [71] That we should be saved from our **enemies**
> And from the hand of all who hate us,

---

64   Liefeld 839.

⁷² To perform the mercy promised to our **fathers**

And to remember His holy **covenant,**
⁷³ The **oath** which He swore to our **father** Abraham:
⁷⁴ To grant us that we,
Being delivered from the hand of our **enemies,**
Might serve Him without fear,
⁷⁵ In holiness and righteousness before Him all the days of our life

First Zacharias blesses or praises God because He "has visited and redeemed His people." The word translated "visited" carries the idea of a charitable visit, like a doctor visiting the sick.[65] By sending Messiah, God "visits" or "comes" to His people to bring what they need—redemption. The same word is used in response to Jesus when He raised the widow's son in Nain (Luke 7:16), and James used it in his definition of true religion (James 1:27). It is also the root word for "visitation" in Luke 19:41-45.

The "horn" represents strength or power, but it also echoes "the horn of David" in Psalm 132:17; salvation from the LORD was to be accomplished by David's Seed, according to "holy prophets" since creation (Hebrews 1:1-2). Verse 71 specifies deliverance from "enemies" and "the hand of all who hate us."

God's salvation or deliverance from enemies is the first of three aspects of His redemptive work; the other two are mercy and faithfulness to His covenant in Genesis 22:16-18. Liefeld emphasizes the political nature of these comments because the Jews were expecting a king who would conquer all earthly enemies and restore David's throne; however, there is also a spiritual element because God had promised Abraham that his seed would bless all nations.[66]

Fulfillment of God's "oath" or "covenant" is at the core of Israel's relationship with God as well as of this song. Even when the Israelites had forsaken God time and again for idols and pleasures of the world, even when they ignored prophet after prophet who begged them to return to God, even when God had allowed Israel and then Judah to be carried into captivity, He had never forgotten his promise. Zacharias calls it "His holy covenant" and "the oath sworn to our father Abraham." Nothing was more sacred to the collective memory of the Jews.

Verses 74-75 state the result of God's faithfulness: Deliverance from enemies brings the opportunity to serve God "without fear" and "in holiness and righteousness" for life. Matthew Henry suggests that verses 73-75 also allude to the sign God gave Moses at the burning bush in Exodus 3:12: "So He said, 'I will certainly be with you. And this shall be a sign to you that I have sent you: When you have brought the people out of Egypt, you shall serve God on this mountain.'"[67]

Part 1 ends on this important note: Deliverance is a two-way street. God saves, but Israel must serve Him.

---

65   Liefeld 840.
66   Liefeld 840.
67   Matthew Henry, *Matthew Henry's Commentary on the Bible*, abridged online. (http://www.biblegateway.com/resources/matthew-henry/Luke.1.67-Luke.1.80).

1. In verses 68 and 78, Zacharias says that God "has visited" His people. As part of His visitation, Jesus performed miracles. What purposes were served by His miracles?

2. In Luke 19:41-44, Jesus wept over Jerusalem's rejection of God's "visitation." How do people react today to the idea that Jesus came down as God to be among people?

Part 2

Having praised God's faithfulness in keeping His covenant, Zacharias now speaks to his newborn son, rejoicing over John's role in Messiah's arrival.

> [76] And you, child, will be called the **prophet** of the Highest;
> For you will go before the face of the Lord to prepare His ways,
> [77] To give knowledge of salvation to His **people**
> By the remission of their sins,
> [78] Through the tender mercy of our God,
> With which the Dayspring from on high has **visited** us;
> [79] To give light to those who sit in darkness and the shadow of death,
> To guide our feet into the way of peace.

Gabriel had told Zacharias that John would go before Messiah "in the spirit and power of Elijah" (Luke 1:17), fulfilling prophecy found in Malachi 3:1 and 4:5. As a prophet of "the Highest," John will be a great servant of God because his purpose and mission are great, as Jesus himself would later confirm (Luke 7:24-28; Matthew 17:10-13). His mission is to "go before, to prepare His ways," so that the people will recognize Jesus and listen to him.

Verses 77-78 emphasize the spiritual element of "salvation" through remission of sins based on God's mercy; John would accomplish his mission by "preaching a baptism of repentance for the remission of sins" (Luke 3:3).

Just Thinking . . .

1. Describe the work of John the Baptist. Why did Jesus describe him as Elijah and as the greatest prophet in Luke 7:24-28?

2. Why did Jesus say, "but he who is least in the kingdom of God is greater than he [John]"?

In verse 78, "Dayspring from on high has visited us" should immediately bring Christ to our minds; John would "bear witness of the Light, that all through him might believe . . . That was the true Light which gives light to every man" (John 1:7-9). "Dayspring" can also be translated "sunrise" (NASB) or "rising sun" (NIV), presenting the imagery of blessed dawn after a long night of fear and despair. When Messiah "visits," He will dispel the darkness of sin and death, as described in Isaiah 60:1-3 and Malachi 4:2.

Gentiles as well as Jews will benefit from the Light as a daily guide "into the way of peace" (v. 79). Christ as Light "guides us into the way of making our peace with God, of keeping up a comfortable communion; that *way of peace* which as sinners we have wandered from and *have not known* nor could ever have known of ourselves."[68]

---

68   Henry (http://www.biblegateway.com/resources/matthew-henry/Luke.1.67-Luke.1.80).

At the conclusion of the song of Zacharias, Luke reports that the child John "grew and became strong in spirit, and was in the deserts till the day of his manifestation to Israel" (v. 80).

Consequences

Whether John's parents lived to witness his bold preaching about Messiah or his death by the hand of King Herod, we do not know. It is obvious by his joyful song, however, that Zacharias understood to some degree the glorious purpose God had for John's life. Zacharias and Elizabeth were delivered *to* serving God by rearing their son to fulfill that purpose; they were delivered *from* the silence of centuries when no prophet had spoken.

In Luke 1:39-45, Elizabeth praises God when she welcomes Mary to her home. Though not a formal song, Elizabeth's words are inspired by the Holy Spirit to express her gratitude to God and to encourage Mary. She reveals great faith and deep joy as she "blesses" Mary and her baby, expressing humility and assuring Mary that the Lord will fulfill all He has told her.

How these two women must have encouraged each other during Mary's visit—praying, planning, and thanking God for trusting them to shape the souls of a great prophet and a greater Savior. As two unique women in all of history, they strengthened each other in present celebration and trusted God for the unknown future when their sons would be bound together in magnificent joy and sorrow to complete the plan of redemption crafted before the beginning of time.

Zacharias, Elizabeth, Mary, and Joseph—ordinary people—will live forever because they allowed God to work His extraordinary, eternal will through their finite lives.

Application: Spread the Word!

Imagine you have just been told the news of a wonderful gift—something you had hoped and prayed for all your life. Now, finally, you learn that you will soon receive this gift. What would be your reaction? Would you remember to thank God? Would you want to tell everyone the good news? Maybe that's how Zacharias felt—eager to praise God and to tell others about his blessing.

Now remember how you felt the day your sins were washed away. How did you feel when you rose from the waters of baptism? Happy? Relieved? Eager to tell everyone of God's love and grace?

For nine months, Zacharias couldn't speak; he couldn't shout praise to God or tell his neighbors of the good news Gabriel had given him. When he obeyed God by naming his son "John," he could finally speak. Perhaps he had thought of what he wanted to say in those long silent months; perhaps his song was spontaneous, born of joy when he saw Elizabeth holding their baby boy.

Either way, his song has a message for us today. God fulfilled His holy covenant by providing both the forerunner of Christ and Christ Himself; He revealed the mystery hidden for ages. As Christians, we have accepted God's deliverance through Christ, but are we fulfilling our part of the covenant? Are we serving Him "without fear / In holiness and righteousness before Him all the days of our life" as Zacharias described? Are we sharing the Good News with others?

With more than seven billion people in the world, we do not lack an audience. Within thirty years of Pentecost, the gospel had been preached to everyone in the known world at that time—and they didn't have television, radio, internet, or mass print media! (Colossians 1:23).

What are we waiting for? Tell someone about Jesus today.

Just Thinking . . .

1. As individual Christians and as congregations of the Lord's church, what are we doing to fulfill the Lord's mission of teaching the gospel to everyone?

2. Can we do more?

Chapter 12

Songs of the Early Church

Ephesians 5:14; 1 Timothy 3:16; 2 Timothy 2:11-13; Jude 24-25

On Any Given Sunday

Lydia wrapped the unleavened bread in a clean cloth. She paused to thank God for the opportunity to prepare the bread and then hurried to finish dressing. Soon the church would gather in her courtyard, and Clement would be among the first to arrive; he would bring the fruit of the vine. How she loved First day—the Lord's day! She saw some of her fellow Christians throughout the week, but when the whole church came together to break bread, when they sang psalms and hymns, she was quite sure she heard angels singing as well.

Today was special; Epaphroditus had just returned to Philippi from Rome, bringing news of Paul and his imprisonment. Lydia knew he had a letter from Paul for the congregation. After they had communed with the Lord, one of the elders would read the letter aloud, slowly and reverently, for Paul wrote by the Spirit's guidance. They might read it twice, savoring every word.

Lydia and the others tried not to worry about Paul, but they couldn't help feeling concern for him and the brave saints who ministered to him. Epaphroditus had been ill in Rome; he nearly died! Thank God he was safe and sound now.

Hearing voices from the courtyard, Lydia hurried to greet her brothers and sisters in Christ. Soon Clement would start a song; the world would fade to a dull background as they gave themselves freely to the worship of God and His Holy Son, Jesus the Christ. Lydia didn't want to miss a single moment!

* * *

In Ephesus, the preacher Timothy reread his lesson once more to be sure he had it well in mind. The church had already heard the entire letter from Paul; now Timothy was taking short passages and discussing them with the members as part of their Lord's Day worship. Eventually, most would commit Paul's inspired words to memory, though they were also copying the letter so that other congregations could benefit from it.

There was a brief but powerful section that Timothy would lead as a song; it began, "God was manifested in the flesh . . . ." The words filled Timothy's heart with awe. God loved people so much that He sent His Son to live and die as a human being. This truth never failed to amaze Timothy.

* * *

So it was, in the first century, that Christians gathered each first day of the week. They met in Jerusalem, Rome, Colossae, Laodicea, Philippi, Corinth, Ephesus, Thessalonica, Lystra, and many other towns and cities—in small villages with forgotten names, on hillsides, under trees, in homes of the members—wherever two or three might gather. When persecution arose, they met secretly or moved to other locations, always teaching and worshiping, sharing copies of the letters from Matthew, Mark, Luke, John, Peter, Paul, James, Jude—letters preserved as Scripture by God and passed down to us.

They prayed together; they read Scripture; they broke bread and drank the fruit of the vine to remember their crucified Savior; they shared their food and clothing with the needy—and they sang. (Based on Acts 16:15,40; 20:7; Ephesians 5:19; Philippians 2:25-30; 1 Timothy 1:3; Revelation 1:10).

Endless Praise

The rich heritage of praising God for His deliverance continues throughout the New Testament. Paul and Silas sang hymns in jail while other prisoners listened (Acts 16:25). Early Christians sang not only to praise God but also to "teach and admonish one another" (Colossians 3:16). In Romans 15:9, Paul quotes from the Song of David in 2 Samuel 22:50 when he speaks of Jews and Gentiles glorifying God together. James suggests Christians should "sing psalms" when they are cheerful (5:13). In Revelation, John describes the singing in heaven so vividly that reading about it makes us long to hear it for ourselves.

When Christians assembled as the church in the first century, they probably drew heavily from the Psalms and prophets for their worship. However, a few passages embedded in the epistles appear to be original songs. We will consider these songs because they refer to the greatest deliverance—the soul's salvation for eternity.

"Arise!" Ephesians 5:14

In Ephesians 5, Paul writes that Christians should walk in love, light, and wisdom as they reject evil by living righteously. When Jesus the Light came into the world, "men loved the darkness rather than the Light, for their deeds were evil" (John 3:19). By His sinless life, however, Jesus rejected and exposed evil; as His people, we should follow His example closely.

Paul elaborates on the need to "walk as children of light" in verses 8-13, then ends with an exhortation that could be a song or chorus:

> [14] Therefore He says:
>
> '**Awake,** you who sleep,
> **Arise** from the dead,
> And **Christ will give you light**.'

The English Standard Version (ESV) reads,

Therefore it says,

> '**Awake**, O sleeper,
> and **arise** from the dead,
> and **Christ will shine** on you.'

These poetic lines are similar in form to Hebrew poetry and songs, and they allude to ideas in Isaiah 26:19 and 60:1, but they are not direct quotations from the Old Testament. Scholars suggest that this verse may be a paraphrase, a quotation from an uninspired source (as in Acts 17:28b), an otherwise unrecorded quotation from Jesus (as in Acts 20:35), or an early Christian hymn.[69]

The song suggests baptism. The sleeper is dead in sin but will arise (resurrect) to "walk in newness of life" (Romans 6:3-4). Christ has already risen from the dead, so He shines or gives light to His followers. In turn, Christians reflect the light of Christ, as the moon reflects sunlight.

---

69   Jay Lockhart, *Ephesians and Philippians,* Truth for Today Commentary, ed. Eddie Cloer, (Searcy, Ar.: Resource Publications, 2009) 263.

We might imagine a group of first-century Christians singing this song as a new babe in Christ rises from the river and is added by the Lord to His church, but there is also a message for mature Christians. We must never forget that Christ has delivered us *from* sin that we might be "children of light" and "lights in the world," and that as light in a dark world, we draw others to the Lord (Ephesians 5:8; Philippians 2:15).

Just Thinking . . .

1. Explain the three-line song in Ephesians 5:14 as it relates to baptism and living the Christian life.

2. Could this song also be used as an exhortation for repentance? How?

"The Mystery of Godliness" 1 Timothy 3:16

At the end of 1 Timothy 3, Paul summarizes his purpose for writing to the young preacher: "I write so that you may know how you ought to conduct yourself in the house of God, which is the church of the living God, the pillar and ground of the truth" (v. 15). In verse 16, he states, "And without controversy great is the mystery of godliness." Then he explains this mystery in the form of a brief hymn.

> God was **manifested** in the flesh,
> **Justified** in the Spirit,
> **Seen** by angels,
> **Preached** among the Gentiles,
> **Believed** on in the world,
> **Received** up in glory.

From the Garden of Eden to the stable in Bethlehem, God's people had wondered when and how He would provide the promised salvation. The mystery has now been revealed in Christ. God manifested—made known or showed Himself—in human flesh as the Man Jesus, the Son of God in Christ. He was justified—made righteous and innocent—by God's Spirit. By performing miracles, Jesus demonstrated His deity (John 3:1-2; 9:30; 20:30-31).

His resurrection proved that God as Father and Holy Spirit accepted the Son's sacrifice for our sins (Romans 4:23-25). He was seen by angels while on the earth, perhaps referring to instances when angels ministered to Him (Matthew 4:11; Luke 22:43). Angels also announced His birth and appeared at His tomb (Luke 2:8-11; Matthew 28:2).

The word translated "Gentiles" here emphasizes God's interest in salvation for all people, not the Jews alone; the same word is translated as "nations" in Matthew 28:19. Concerning 1 Timothy 3:16, one commentary notes that "what was preached was not a theory or even a creed, but a Person."[70] Christ is the message preached—proclaimed—to everyone (1 Corinthians 1:23). When He was preached, people believed on Him—had faith and trust in Him. Faithful preaching produces obedient faith (Romans 10:14-15).

Finally, He was received up in glory as He ascended to heaven after His earthly ministry was complete (Acts 1:2). In a six-line hymn, Paul by the Holy Spirit captures the essentials of Christ's identity from birth to ascension. Earle concludes, "Preaching Christ means preaching his life, death, resurrection, and ascension as the glorified Lord."[71]

Christians are delivered *to* living for Christ—the Son of God Who lives eternally.

---

70   Ralph Earle, "1 and 2 Timothy" in *Ephesians through Philemon*, The Expositor's Bible Commentary, ed. Frank E. Gaebelein, vol. 11 (Grand Rapids, Mich.: Zondervan, 1981) 370.

71   Earle 370.

People often speak of the "mystery" of Christianity as if no one knows it, yet Paul explains this mystery in 1 Timothy 3:16. Briefly state the meaning of "the mystery of godliness" based on this verse.

"A Faithful Saying" 2 Timothy 2:11-13

Paul includes another short poem thought to be a first-century hymn in his second letter to Timothy. It follows comments about enduring trouble and imprisonment for preaching the gospel, assuring fellow Christians that though Paul is in chains, "the word of God is not chained" (vv. verses 9-10). Then he writes,

[11] This is a faithful saying:

For if we **died** with Him,
We shall also **live** with Him.

[12] If we **endure**,
We shall also **reign** with Him.
If we **deny** Him,
He also will **deny** us.

[13] If we are **faithless,**
He remains **faithful;**
He cannot **deny** Himself.

The hymn consists of an introductory statement declaring faithfulness, four "if" clauses coupled with their conclusions, and a closing statement that repeats the fourth conclusion. Two couplets are positive; they encourage by reviewing God's promises. Two are negative; they warn against unfaithfulness.

Each couplet highlights an action and a result. Dying with Christ occurs in baptism; the result is life in Christ on this earth as well as in eternity. Christians are dead to sin but alive to God in Christ Jesus (Romans 6:3-6, 8, 11). Endurance of persecution leads to the rewards of salvation and reigning in heaven with Christ (Matthew 10:22; Revelation 2:10).

On the negative side, if we deny Christ, He will deny us (Matthew 10:33). Denying Christ suggests unbelief and disobedience; those who deny Him become faithless. Yet in the face of rejection, Christ remains faithful. He does not lower the standard or excuse our denial. This last concept is important enough to warrant emphatic repetition: Christ cannot deny Himself.

Paul lived in perilous times and suffered persecution frequently, yet he never failed to preach and practice faithful endurance. He knew what unbelievers couldn't grasp, that to live is Christ and to die is gain, that living without Christ is far worse than dying for Him. This song reminds us that Christians are delivered *from* sin and delivered *to* salvation and eternal glory by way of persecution endured. Again, we must live in and for Christ.

Just Thinking . . .

1. Does 2 Timothy 2:11-13 apply to Christians today? How does persecution affect individuals and the church? How was Paul persecuted? Consider 2 Corinthians 11:20-28.

2. Though we may not suffer physical persecution that would tempt us to deny Christ, is it possible that we could deny Christ, either consciously or unconsciously, by the way we live our lives? How?

"Glory . . . Now and Forever" Jude 24-25

The Book of Jude is known for strong warnings against false teachers and the exhortation "to contend earnestly for the faith which was once for all delivered to the saints" (v. 3). He also emphasizes the Christian's responsibility to maintain and grow spiritually by prayer and by remaining in the love of God as he/she looks to (anticipates) Christ in eternity (vv. verses 20-21).

Then Jude ends his letter with beautiful praise, encouraging us to remember that we are not alone in our effort to remain faithful.

> [24] Now to **Him who is able to keep you from stumbling,**
> And **to present you faultless**
> Before the presence of His glory with exceeding joy,
> [25] **To God our Savior,**
> Who alone is wise,
> Be **glory and majesty,**
> **Dominion and power,**
> Both now and forever.
> Amen (Jude 24-25).

Jude first addresses God as "Him who is able to keep you from stumbling." This doesn't mean that Christians will never stumble or sin; rather, it means our relationship with God in Christ will strengthen and help us as we walk in the light of His word. He will "present you faultless/Before the presence of His glory" by His cleansing blood (Romans 5:8-9; Ephesians 5: 25-27; 1:7). Duane Warden comments, "The assurance is that the one who will put his faith in Christ, who will keep looking to Him for guidance, who will repent and turn from sin—this one will stand."[72]

In verse 25, Jude writes "To God our Savior." The American Standard Version (ASV) and ESV include "through Jesus Christ our Lord" after "To God our Savior;" the New International Version (NIV) includes it later in the verse. This is not a contradiction; Father, Son, and Holy Spirit comprise One God (Genesis 1:2,26; John 1:1-3; 10:29-31).

To God "Who alone is wise," Jude attributes four other qualities: "glory, majesty, dominion, and power." "Glory" describes God's magnificence; Blum suggests the synonyms "radiance" or "moral splendor." Then "majesty" describes God's greatness.[73]

"Dominion and power" speak of God's sovereignty and authority as well as His mighty strength, as we have seen in other songs. "Both now and forever" reminds us that God doesn't change. He is still "able" to carry out His plans, as He always has been and always will be (Isaiah 46:9-10).

Blum writes, "Salvation is completely secure because God's own purpose stands and because he is able to do all that he wills."[74]

---

72   Duane Warden, *1 and 2 Peter and Jude,* Truth for Today Commentary, ed. Eddie Cloer, (Searcy, Ar.: Resource Publications, 2009) 512.
73   Edwin A. Blum, "Jude" in *Hebrews through Revelation,* The Expositor's Bible Commentary, ed. Frank E. Gaebelein, vol. 12 (Grand Rapids, Mich.: Zondervan, 1981) 396.
74   Blum 396.

Just Thinking . . .

1. Jude has harsh words regarding false teachers. Describe the change in tone in the last two verses.

2. Review the songs in this chapter and discuss them in light of the instructions for singing in Ephesians 5:19 and Colossians 3:16.

3. These brief songs are very different from the Song of Moses or the Song of Deborah. Why should they be included as songs of deliverance?

Application: Sing On!

Other New Testament passages that may be hymns of praise include John 1:1-18 and Philippians 2:5-11. Both present the nature of Christ as equal with God yet also fully human while on earth.[75] John's lyrical introduction rolls eloquently from the tongue when read aloud; how powerful it would be if it were set to music. When Paul exhorts the Philippians to "have the mind of Christ," he presents a dramatic contrast between the humility and exaltation of Christ. Study these passages in light of comments made about songs of deliverance.

Just Thinking . . .

1. Select several hymns in the songbook your congregation uses and discuss them in terms of these questions:

   - Are there any songs of deliverance?

   - Do the most frequently used songs glorify God?

   - Do the words bring to mind Christ's sacrifice?

   - Do they inspire righteous living, holiness, faith, obedience, and other principles found in Scripture?

   - Do any of the songs "teach and admonish"?

2. How can our singing be a "sacrifice of praise" for God's continual deliverance? (Hebrews 13:15).

---

75   Stan Mitchell, *Give the Winds a Mighty Voice: Our Worship in Song* (Winona, Miss.: J.C. Choate Publications, 2000) 53.

Chapter 13
Five Songs of Heaven in Revelation
Revelation 4:8, 11; 5:9-10, 12, 13b; 7:12; 11:17-18; 15:3-4

"There's a Great Day Coming"

Jesus is coming back. He said, "Be ready, for only the Father knows when." It may be early morning or bright noon or dark midnight. People will be doing everyday things—eating, drinking, getting married. Trumpets will sound; the archangel will shout. Jesus will come with glory, holy angels, and fire to melt the familiar elements of earth; the heavens will dissolve. There will be a new heaven and a new earth.

The dead will rise; the living will be caught up with them. God's people will be changed in the twinkling of an eye, shaking off dusty mortality and slipping into something incorruptible—something barely imaginable now—immortality. Death and the fear of it will be swallowed up in victory.

There will be judgment, a sorting out of sheep and goats, righteous and unrighteous, a just assignment of everlasting reward or everlasting punishment. Every person who has ever lived will stand before the Lord—no excuses, no second chances, no escape. Those who are not found in Christ will be lost forever. God will exact His vengeance on those who don't know him and don't obey the gospel of Christ.

The righteous will hear, "Well done, good and faithful servant; enter into the joy of your lord." Eternal worship at God's throne will begin, the beauty of holiness, the spiritual consummation that Christians long to know. Be ready; He is coming. (Based on Matthew 24:36-44; 25:21, 31-46; 1 Corinthians15:48-58; 1 Thessalonians 4:15-17; 5:2; 2 Thessalonians 1:6-10; 2 Peter 3:10-14).

Heavenly Songs of Deliverance

Angels announced the birth of Jesus with praise and glory from the heavens, but at the cross, there was no song.

At the empty tomb, there was no song.

In heaven, however, there will be singing—glorious, perfect, endless praise for God and joyous celebration of His victory over sin. John's preview of heaven in Revelation challenges and exhilarates the Christian's imagination and soul. This chapter doesn't offer an in-depth study of Revelation; instead, our purpose is to consider five passages that express praise in heavenly worship.

For ease of reference, we call these passages "songs," though not all are designated as such, but all express adoration, acknowledgment, and worship of God for providing the Way of salvation and the eternal home for those saved. Heaven as our home forever is the ultimate deliverance.

"Holy, Holy, Holy"

Revelation 4:8, 11

Keep in mind that Revelation was written to Christians who were suffering severe persecution around A.D. 94-96 from the Roman Emperor Domitian, and the theme of the book is "victorious Christianity."[76] In

---

76 David L. Roper, *Revelation 1-11,* Truth for Today Commentary, ed. Eddie Cloer, (Searcy, Ar.: Resource

the battle between good and evil that began in the Garden of Eden, good wins. God wins, and by extension, those who belong to God also win. Evil emperors, generals, or dictators may appear to be in control, but God's purpose will triumph in the end. He reveals this truth to the apostle John not only for the benefit of persecuted Christians during Roman rule but also for the generations to come.

Revelation 4 presents a vision of God on His throne that should "dazzle the eyes and stagger the imagination" and "make us marvel at the magnificence of God."[77]

John writes in verse 3 that God appears like jasper and sardius stone, and a rainbow around the throne is like an emerald. Encircling God's throne are twenty-four smaller thrones where twenty-four elders sit, wearing white robes and golden crowns (v. 4). These elders aren't identified by name or title; "elders" simply suggests aged men. Four living creatures, each with six wings and "full of eyes around and within," never rest from praising (verses 6-8). Thunder and lightning come from God's throne.

The setting for the thrones, the elders, and the living creatures is something "like a sea of glass, like crystal," (v. 6). Imagine the glitter and gleam from the crystal-like substance, from the white robes, and from the flashes of lightning, not to mention the appearance of God, Light personified, for this vision brings John and those who read his revelation into the very presence of God the Creator.

Following this dramatic description, verse 8 presents the continual praise from the four living creatures:

> **Holy, holy, holy**,
> Lord God Almighty,
> Who **was** and **is** and **is to come**!

Repeating the word "holy" three times declares the highest degree of holiness—God is the purest, most sacred Being. "Lord" means "ruler." "Almighty" defines His complete, infinite power. Line 3 celebrates His eternal existence—God has no beginning or end—and His permanent involvement in the past, present, and future.[78]

While the living creatures honor "Him who sits on the throne," the elders fall down in worship, casting their crowns before Him (verses 9-10). They sing,

> You are worthy, O Lord,
> To receive **glory** and **honor** and **power**;
> For You created all things,
> And by Your will they exist and were created (v. 11).

In ancient times, conquered kings surrendered their crowns in humiliation to the conqueror; these elders cast down their crowns as symbols of spiritual victory as they gratefully acknowledge that God gave them the victory.[79] This brief hymn announces heaven's great theme song—praise in worship of God because He deserves all recognition and gratitude for who He is and what He has done.

Publications, 2002) 6, 52.

77   Roper 206.

78   Alan Johnson, "Revelation" in *Hebrews through Revelation,* The Expositor's Bible Commentary, ed. Frank E. Gaebelein, vol. 12 (Grand Rapids, Mich.: Zondervan, 1981) 463.

79   Roper 217.

David Roper comments, "In the original text, each of the words glory, honor, and power is preceded by the definite article (the)—implying that God alone is worthy of these expressions of praise."[80] By His "will" and His spoken word, God created the world; His creation continues to exist as long as He wills (Genesis 1:3; John 1:1-2).

God sustains and reconciles the world by His will and through Jesus (Colossians 1:13-20).God will destroy the world in His time (2 Peter 3:3-10). Persecution will end; the world will pass away; God always remains worthy of praise.

Just Thinking . . .

1. In Revelation 4:8, what does the repetition of the word "holy" indicate about the character of God? Compare this song with the one found in most hymnals, "Holy, Holy, Holy," by Reginald Heber.

2. Why is God alone worthy to receive "glory and honor and power" in 4:11? How do we "give" these qualities to God in our worship?

"A New Song"

Revelation 5:9-10, 12, 13b

In Revelation 5, John sees a scroll with seven seals in God's right hand. John weeps because "no one was found worthy to open and read the scroll," but an elder reassures him: "Behold, the Lion of the tribe of Judah, the Root of David, has prevailed to open the scroll" (vv. verses 1-5). He speaks of the human ancestry of Messiah (Genesis 49:8-11; Isaiah 11:1,10).

Then John sees a Lamb Who looks as if He had been slain—Christ, sacrificed, dead, but now alive forever and glorified. When He takes the scroll, the living creatures and the elders fall down before Him. They hold harps and golden bowls of incense, representing praise and prayers of the saints (vv. verses 8-9).

> [9] And they sang a new song, saying:
>
> **You are worthy** to take the scroll,
> And to open its seals;
> For **You were slain**,
> And have **redeemed** us to God by Your **blood**
> Out of every tribe and tongue and people and nation,
> [10] And have made us kings and priests to our God;
> And we shall reign on the earth.

The song is "new" since it could not be sung before Messiah completed His mission of redemption. Before He died, Jesus said, "It is finished" (John 19:30). The Lamb is worthy because He was slain. The Greek word "sphazo" translated "slain" means "to butcher . . . especially an animal for food or sacrifice."[81] God's people are redeemed by the sacrifice of the Lamb's blood.

---

80   Roper 217.

81   *Strong's Concordance with Hebrew and Greek Lexicon* online: "sphazo" #4969. www.eliyah.com/lexicon.html

Those redeemed are from every tribe (family group), tongue (linguistic group), people (social group), and nation (ethnic group), representing all humanity.[82] The redeemed have also become "kings and priests to our God" (1 Peter 2:9). Victory is implied by "shall reign;" Christians persecuted in the first century needed to hear that even if they died for Christ, they would be victorious.[83]

Many angels surround the throne and join in: "and the number of them was ten thousand times ten thousand, and thousands of thousands," saying loudly,

> Worthy is the Lamb who was slain
> To receive **power** and **riches** and **wisdom**,
> And **strength** and **honor** and **glory** and **blessing**! (v. 12).

Having established the Lamb's worthiness, the singers describe what the Lamb is worthy to receive. "All these are intrinsic qualities of Christ, except the last, which is the expression of the creatures' worship: 'praise' or 'blessing.'"[84]

Could this song become any louder or grander? Yes! In verse 13 John writes, "And every creature which is in heaven and on the earth and under the earth and such as are in the sea, and all that are in them, I heard saying,"

> **Blessing** and **honor** and **glory** and **power**
> Be to Him who sits on the throne,
> And **to the Lamb**, forever and ever! (v. 13b).

Amen!

The crescendo increases as all creation joins in; "everything everywhere" praises God and Christ the Lamb, for they are One![85]

The NASB translates verse 14 as "And the four living creatures kept saying, 'Amen.'" Perhaps they said "amen" at the end of each line, for emphasis. The twenty-four elders once more fall before the throne in worship and glorious praise with creation.

Just Thinking . . .

1. In Revelation 5:9, why is the song "new"? Who sings it?

2. Who is the Lamb in 5:12 and why is He the only person worthy to open the scroll?

3. We mentioned earlier that only God is worthy to receive glory, honor, and power, yet 5:12 says that the Lamb is also worthy to receive these blessings. What does that tell us about the relationship between God and Christ?

4. In class, ask three people to read aloud Revelation 5:9-10. Add five more voices, so that eight are reading together verse 12. Then ask the rest of the class to join in and read verse 13. Read the verses again as suggested, but have the whole class say "amen" after each verse. What is the effect?

---

82   Roper 235.
83   Roper 236.
84   Johnson 470.
85   Roper 238.

"Salvation!"

Revelation 7:12

In Revelation 7, John sees another group in God's throne room, "a great multitude which no one could number, of all nations, peoples, and tongues, standing before the throne and before the Lamb, clothed with white robes, with palm branches in their hands" (v. 9). In verse 10, they shout, **"Salvation belongs to our God who sits on the throne, and to the Lamb!"**

These people rightly announce that God is the source of salvation; He sent His Son Jesus to offer salvation to humanity (Matthew 1:21; Romans 1:16; Titus 2:11-12). Eternal life in heaven is salvation's final stage—called "salvation ready to be revealed in the last time" in 1 Peter 1:4-5. Angels, the four living creatures, and the twenty-four elders fall again before the throne in worship, saying,

> **Amen!** Blessing and glory and wisdom,
> **Thanksgiving and honor and power and might,**
> Be to our God forever and ever.
> **Amen** (v. 12).

The word "amen" has the same meaning in Hebrew, Greek, and English: "sure, true; so be it." In the King James Version (KJV), the word translated "verily" before many statements by Jesus is from the Greek "am-ane" of Hebrew origin; its use re-enforced the truth of words spoken before or after it.[86]

"Amen" brackets this brief song, testifying to the truth about salvation and ending the song emphatically. The song itself repeats the seven-fold tribute to the Lamb in Revelation 5:12 with three differences: 1) different word order, 2) "thanksgiving" replaces "riches," and 3) "the" precedes each word here in the original text but not in 5:12.[87] The song reaffirms God's greatness and generosity.

After the song, an elder asks John if he knows this multitude; John defers, "Sir, you know." The elder explains that these people "come out of the great tribulation." Because they were faithful under persecution, they wear robes made white by the Lamb's blood, and they have the honor of serving God "day and night," meaning "always."

Their reward is great; God will "dwell among them;" the Lamb "will shepherd them" to "living fountains of waters;" and "God will wipe away every tear from their eyes" (vv. verses 14-17). First-century Christians enduring persecution needed to know their ultimate deliverance would be eternal life with God and freedom from all earthly woes!

"God's Kingdom Proclaimed"

Revelation 11:17-18

In Revelation 11, God as Creator and Redeemer is now praised as a Conquering King. After the seventh trumpet sounds, unidentified loud voices say, "The kingdoms of this world have become the kingdoms of our Lord and of His Christ, and He shall reign forever and ever!" (v. 15).

God has always reigned over His creation, but this passage previews the time to come when God's people will celebrate the victory of God's purpose and all people will acknowledge God's sovereignty (Romans 14:9-12).[88] Once more, the twenty-four elders fall on their faces and worship God:

---

86   *Strong's Hebrew and Greek Lexicon* online: "am-ane" #281. www.eliyah.com/lexicon.html
87   Roper 309-310.
88   Roper 309-310.

> We give You thanks, O Lord God Almighty,
> The One who is and who was and who is to come,
> Because **You have taken Your great power and reigned.**
> [18] The **nations were angry**, and **Your wrath has come,**
> And the time of the dead, that they should be judged,
> And that You should **reward** Your servants the prophets and the saints,
> And those who fear Your name, small and great,
> And should **destroy** those who destroy the earth (vv. verses 17-18).

The oldest manuscripts of Revelation don't have the phrase "who is to come" in this song, so the more recent translations such as the ESV, NASB and NIV don't include it.[89] Its absence doesn't contradict God's eternal existence. John sees a vision of the future as if it has already come; he sees what the end-of-the-world-as-we-know-it-forever-reign-of-God looks like. Because He is outside of time, God is already victorious. For us, the events celebrated in this song are still in the future.

When God reveals His final, official reign, the nations react with anger because He overthrows their willful disregard for His purposes.[90] Their anger, however, is nothing compared to God's wrath. The time has come for judgment, punishment, and reward. All who are faithful to God and fear His name will be rewarded. Those who destroy the earth will be destroyed.

The Greek word translated "destroy" means "corrupt or decay" here. "The Spirit was speaking of those who have corrupted this earth—those who have filled it with moral filth, blasphemous error, and godless unbelief."[91] First-century Rome was corrupt, but so is our modern society. When we feel overwhelmed by the evil, we should feel encouraged by this song. Deliverance is certain.

These verses don't teach that God ceased to reign for a time but will reign again. God has always reigned over His creation; He is still ruling today, though many do not acknowledge His rulership. Neither do these verses teach that when Christ returns, He will set up an earthly kingdom. Instead, this song teaches that someday all people will acknowledge God's sovereignty (Romans 14:11); those who rejected His reign will be punished. Briefly, this song celebrates God's ultimate victory.[92]

Just Thinking . . .

1. Why would first-century Christians under persecution have found comfort in Revelation 11:17-18?

2. Is there comfort in these verses for us today? Why or why not?

"Of Moses and the Lamb"

(Revelation 15:3-4)

Finally, we will consider the Song of Moses and the Song of the Lamb in Revelation 15—two names but one song of deliverance. This song resonates with the faithful from Old Testament times as well as with Jewish and Gentile Christians from the first century to the present day. Moses, God's servant, and the Lamb, God's Son, each led the people of God from bondage to freedom, from sin to salvation. The ancient rabbis called Moses and Messiah "the first deliverer and the last Deliverer."[93]

89   Roper 447.

90   Roper 450.

91   Roper 452.

92   Roper 448-449.

93   Martin H. Franzmann, *he Revelation to John* (St. Louis, Mo.: Concordia Publishing House, 1976) 105.

The Song of Moses and the Lamb should sound familiar; every line contains phrases from other psalms and the prophets. Such repetition connects the praise and faith of God's people throughout the ages and testifies to God's consistent, ageless character and purpose.

Before he hears the song, John sees "something like a sea of glass mingled with fire." Here all who were faithful unto death stand victorious, holding harps and singing (Revelation 15:2; cf. 2:10). Some think this sea is a spiritual symbol of the Red Sea; the faithful stand on or by it as the Israelites stood safely on the eastern shore of the Red Sea. Now all who have been delivered by God sing triumphantly in His presence.[94] The song spans history from the time of Moses until the Judgment Day in John's vision.

> [3]**Great** and **marvelous** are Your works,
> Lord God Almighty!
> **Just** and **true** are Your ways,
> O King of the saints!
> [4] Who shall not fear You, O Lord, and glorify Your name?
> For You alone are **holy.**
> For **all nations** shall come and worship before You,
> For Your **judgments have been manifested.**

The singers address God personally, praising His works, His ways, and His name. He is described in superlatives that are summarized by the name "Lord God Almighty." Feared and glorified, He is "King of the saints." (Other translations: "ages" and "nations"). He is and always has been Lord and King over everyone and everything.

Because of what God has done and who He is, all nations will worship Him once His judgments have been made known. On Judgment Day, no one will doubt God's holy character or omnipotence or sovereignty; all will worship and wait for just judgment.

Some assume that since all nations will worship God, all will be saved. Such an assumption contradicts the description of God's justice in Revelation 11:18 as well as the teaching of Christ in Matthew 25 and in numerous passages throughout the New Testament.

Acknowledging God is not the same as obeying Him. While we live on earth, we have the opportunity to hear and obey the gospel; then we must remain faithful. Paul pleaded with the Corinthian church "not to receive the grace of God in vain" and added, "Behold, now is the accepted time; behold, now is the day of salvation" (2 Corinthians 6:1-2). John envisions a time when those who rejected Christ in this life will acknowledge Him, but it will be too late to obey.

Just Thinking . . .

1. Compare the language in the Song of Moses and the Lamb in Revelation 15 with these references: Exodus 15:12,13; Deuteronomy 32:4; Psalm 92:5; 98:1; 139:14; 145:17; 99:3; 111:9; 1 Samuel 2:2; Jeremiah 10:7; Amos 4:13; Psalm 86:9; 98:2.

2. What do the similarities tell us about God and the people who wrote these songs?

Application: Anticipation

"Everybody wants to go to heaven, but nobody wants to die." So goes the old adage that may be too true for comfort. Then there is, "I want to go to heaven—but not yet." Today, many Christians are so comfortable here on earth, heaven has little or no appeal. Only when we contrast the immoral, atheistic, decaying world around us with the matchless beauty and purity of heaven will we truly anticipate heaven.

94   Roper 135-136.

As Christians waiting to achieve the final victory over death, what do we anticipate? Consider the following:

- hearing and singing "new songs" in heaven;

- deliverance *from* mortality with all its shackles and suffering;

- deliverance *to* immortality, eternal praise, worship, and service to the Creator and the Lamb;

- worship before God's throne with other saints from every nation and age of human history;

- reunion with loved ones;

- most of all, eternal life with Jesus.

May we live our lives today with eternity in mind; may we praise Him now for all He has done, knowing He will bring to completion the work He has begun in us (Philippians 1:6).

> [20] Now may the God of peace who brought up our Lord Jesus from the dead, that great Shepherd of the sheep, through the blood of the everlasting covenant, [21] make you complete in every good work to do His will, working in you what is well pleasing in His sight, through Jesus Christ, to whom *be* glory forever and ever. Amen (Hebrews 13:20-21).

There's a great day coming. Be ready! Amen. Come, Lord Jesus.

Just Thinking . . .

1. On Judgment Day, everyone will worship God. Does this mean that even atheists and infidels will be saved? (Matthew 10:27-28; 23:33; Luke 16:19-31; 2 Thessalonians 1:3-10; 2 Peter 2:1-17).

2. Memorize short passages from your favorite songs of deliverance in this study. Let these passages encourage in times of stress, illness, temptation, or fear.

3. Look for modern hymns or praise songs that echo the ideas in the songs of deliverance.

Works Cited

Archer, Jr., Gleason L. "Daniel" in *Daniel and the Minor Prophets*. The Expositor's Bible Commentary, ed. Frank E. Gaebelein, vol.7. Grand Rapids, Mich.: Zondervan, 1985.

Blum, Edwin A. "Jude" in *Hebrews through Revelation*. The Expositor's Bible Commentary, ed. Frank E. Gaebelein, vol.12. Grand Rapids, Mich.: Zondervan, 1981.

Cloer, Eddie. *Psalms 1-50*. Truth for Today Commentary, ed. Eddie Cloer. Searcy, Ar.: Resource Publications, 2005.

Earle, Ralph. "1 and 2 Timothy" in *Ephesians through Philemon*. The Expositor's Bible Commentary, ed. Frank E. Gaebelein, vol.11. Grand Rapids, Mich.: Zondervan, 1981.

Ellison, H.L. "Jonah" in *Daniel and the Minor Prophets*. The Expositor's Bible Commentary, ed. Frank E. Gaebelein, vol.7. Grand Rapids, Mich.: Zondervan, 1985.

Franzmann, Martin H. *The Revelation to John*. St. Louis, Mo.: Concordia Publishing House, 1976.

Henry, Matthew. *Matthew Henry's Commentary on the Bible*. Abridged online at (http://www.biblegateway.com/resources/matthew-henry/Luke.1.67-Luke.1.80).

Heschel, Abraham. *The Prophets*. Peabody, Mass.: Prince Press, an imprint of Hendrickson Publishers, 2001.

Johnson, Alan. "Revelation" in *Hebrews through Revelation*. The Expositor's Bible Commentary, ed. Frank E. Gaebelein, vol.12. Grand Rapids, Mich.: Zondervan, 1981.

Kaiser, Jr., Walter C. "Exodus" in *Genesis, Exodus, Leviticus and Numbers*. The Expositor's Bible Commentary, ed. Frank E. Gaebelein, vol. 2. Grand Rapids, Mich.; Zondervan, 1990.

Liefeld, Walter L. "Luke" in *Matthew, Mark, Luke*. The Expositor's Bible Commentary, ed. Frank E. Gaebelein, vol.7. Grand Rapids, Mich.: Zondervan, 1986.

Lockhart, Jay. *Ephesians and Philippians*. Truth for Today Commentary, ed. Eddie Cloer. Searcy, Ar.: Resource Publications, 2009.

Olmstead, Albert Ten Eyck. *History of Assyria*. New York: Charles Scribner's Sons, 1923.

Rawlinson, G. *Psalms*. The Pulpit Commentary, ed. H.D.M. Spence and Joseph S. Exell, vol.8. Grand Rapids, Mich.: Wm. B. Eerdmans Publishing Co., 1950.

Roper, David L. *Revelation 1-11*. Truth for Today Commentary, ed. Eddie Cloer. Searcy, Ar.: Resource Publications, 2002.

Smith. R. Payne. "2 Samuel" in *Ruth, 1 Samuel and 2 Samuel*. The Pulpit Commentary, ed. H.D.M. Spence and Joseph S. Exell, vol4. Grand Rapids, Mich.: Wm. B. Eerdmans Publishing Co., 1950.

Strong, James. *Strong's Concordance with Hebrew and Greek Lexicon*. Online at www.eliyah.com/lexicon.html.

Thompson. J.R. "Jonah" in *Amos-Malachi*. The Pulpit Commentary, ed. H.D.M. Spence and Joseph S. Exell, vol.14. Grand Rapids, Mich.: Wm. B. Eerdmans Publishing Co. 1950.

Warden, Duane. *1 and 2 Peter and Jude*. Truth for Today Commentary, ed. Eddie Cloer. Searcy, Ar.: Resource Publications, 2009.

Wolf, Herbert. "Judges" in *Deuteronomy, Joshua, Judges, Ruth, 1 and 2 Samuel*. The Expositor's Bible Commentary, ed. Frank E. Gaebelein, vol.3. Grand Rapids, Mich.: Zondervan, 1992.

Youngblood, Ronald R. "1 and 2 Samuel" in *Deuteronomy, Joshua, Judges, Ruth, 1 and 2 Samuel*. The Expositor's Bible Commentary, ed. Frank. E. Gaebelein, vol. 3. Grand Rapids, Mich.: Zondervan, 1992.

Other Books by Debra Griffin Mitchell

Ladies' class studies published by J.C. Choate Publications are available from Choate Publications in Winona, Miss., or from the author. Contact her at mitchelld@bellsouth.net

Blessed beyond Measure. This 13-lesson study of Christian blessings includes a "blessing workshop" to help you personalize the lessons and become more aware of your blessings in Christ.

First Sisters. What can we learn from our first sisters—the women described in Acts—and their contributions to the first-century church? Read about Mary, Lydia, Dorcas, and other women we should imitate as they imitated Christ.

Self-published books available from the author at mitchelldj@bellsouth.net

A Flame before the Lord. This novel is based on the life of Hannah and her son Samuel, the last judge and prophet who was guided by God to anoint the first two kings of Israel—Saul and David. It is available on amazon.com under Debra Figgins Griffin or from the author.

The Teddy Bear File: A Novel of Murder and Forgiveness. In this contemporary novel with Christian themes, Jamie Meyers searches for her father's murderer and learns to help victims of False Memory Syndrome. It is available on amazon.com under Debra Figgins Griffin or from the author.

The Death Bet: Another Jamie Meyers Mystery. Jamie helps a friend whose life is in danger and discovers her own spiritual needs. (Temporarily out of print)

Stranded in September: Life Writing. This collection of poetry and stories is available on amazon.com under Debra Griffin Mitchell.

Biography

Debra Griffin Mitchell is a writer and teacher who loves to study and share God's word. Born in Caruthersville, Missouri, she graduated from Crowley's Ridge College in 1970 and Oklahoma Christian College in 1971. She also completed a master's degree in English and a specialist degree in community college teaching from Arkansas State University.

Debra and her husband Bill Griffin, Jr., worked with local congregations of the Lord's church in several states. They also taught in public schools and community colleges before his death in 2000.

In 2004, Debra married long-time missionary to Zimbabwe, Loy Mitchell, whose first wife died in 2002. Each year Loy and Debra return to Zimbabwe to preach and teach. Currently, they work with the Knott church of Christ in Knott, Texas. Between them they have five children, sixteen grandchildren, and six great-grandchildren.

Other Books by WVBS Publishing

Printed copies of these books are available from your local Christian bookstore or wvbs.org

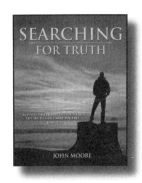

This 112-page, full-color study guide, written by John Moore, is a great resource as a companion to the Searching for Truth DVD, or used on its own as a workbook. The material is suitable for individual study or used in any Bible class setting.

The study guide includes the extended question sections, including a "Section Review" after each section and a "Chapter Review" at the end of each chapter. To close-out the chapter there is a "Digging Deeper" section, which includes additional verses on the subject matter that are not used in the text. The answer to every question can be found in the Answer Key section at the end of the book.

This beautiful, 132-page, full-color book makes a wonderful teaching tool and gift for anyone who would like to study these subjects: Tattoos, Gambling, Drinking, Dancing, Lying, Modesty, Pornography, Marriage Divorce and Remarriage, and What Must I Do To Be Saved? These are subjects that every person needs to study, in order to understand how these subjects can impact their lives spiritually and physically.

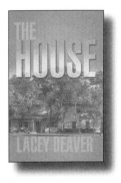

This new faith-based Christian-fiction book is a full-color, 187-page printed version of the story used in the movie "Bound." Reviewers of this book have described it as "captivating," agreeing that they were unable to put it down once they started reading it.

The story is about a young woman whose life has been tormented with struggle and bad choices. A set of unforeseen circumstances finds her the reluctant guest of a family who helps her face the important decisions in her life. With her heart wounded by grief, unlikely friends come to the rescue. They help Cheri find the hope and the truth that will forever change her life.

Many forces in our culture have declared war on our young men. *Men in the Making* is a bold new book that empowers young men to be pure and brave as they stand strong against the destructive forces of Satan. Every teenage boy must learn to embrace his God-given responsibilities and the roles that only he can fill. *Men in the Making* provides a framework that helps young men learn to honor the older, protect the weak, overcome sexual temptations, control their tongues, and stand for the Truth. If you are looking for a way to make tomorrow's world a better place, give this book to every teenage boy you know and encourage him to read it earnestly.

This is a full-color, 92-page book for every young man from 12- to 20-years-old. Within the pages of this book the authors have taken on the task of sharing the wisdom they have gleaned becoming and being men of God. Their candid insights will help every young man. In addition, the book is filled with many references to great teaching sources located for free online, or on other DVDs and books.